ALL THINGS NEW

These delightfully crafted essays will spark in you a fresh desire to glorify God by visiting an art gallery, watching a classic movie, reading a work of literature at a leisurely pace or listening to some of the great music of the past. They may, in fact, stir you to write a hymn yourself, or pick up a paint brush, a pen or a camera...

PETER PIKKERT, professor of missions and theology at Cornerstone College, The Netherlands, and author of several books including *The Epic of God and Man*.

In the past century or so, if there has been an area of weakness in evangelical witness, it has been in relation to the aesthetic world of the arts. Though we have been quick to affirm Christ's lordship over all of life, the truth of the matter is that we have been extremely slow to apply this to the arts. And we have thus been hampered in answering one of the great questions of life: What is beauty? This collection of essays by Jeremy W. Johnston helpfully tackles this neglected area of Christian thought head-on and in so doing forces us to realize what we have been missing and how we should now go about recovering this lost dimension of Christian reflection. An extremely helpful book.

MICHAEL A.G. HAYKIN, professor of church history and biblical spirituality and director of The Andrew Fuller Center for Baptist Studies at The Southern Baptist Theological Seminary in Louisville, Kentucky

In *All Things New: Essays on Christianity, culture & the arts*, writer Jeremy W. Johnston leads readers on a wide-ranging romp through the arts. He argues solidly how the arts can help and encourage faith, and how faith can nurture the arts. Readers are challenged to develop "a biblical and God glorifying appreciation of beauty—a Christian aesthetic." I like that Johnston recognizes we mere humans are commanded to create, and so we should take that risk. This collection of essays, perfect for picking up and dipping into time and again, encourages us to recite poetry, gobble up great novels, wander through galleries, delight in gourmet food and see the fingerprint of the Creative One in all things good and beautiful."

KAREN STILLER, senior editor, *Faith Today* magazine

As a fine artist who enjoys reading on art history and theological aesthetics, I found Jeremy W. Johnston to possess an excellent grasp of an embodied and holistic approach to Christian engagement with the arts. The reader will find this collection of essays, written in a succinct and approachable style, to offer a helpful framework for discerning the messages conveyed in literature, film, visual art, music and modern culture as a whole. Johnston strikes a wonderful balance between respecting artistic tradition and doctrine but also recognizing how the Master Artist is always up to 'doing a new thing' in our world, through which the arts can usher in streams of life-giving water, quenching the dry wasteland of pragmatism within and outside of the church.

JOSH TIESSEN, award-winning fine artist and Associate Living Master

In this collection of essays, Jeremy W. Johnston shows that the God who made us calls us to also be makers, to be artists of both the fine and the domestic arts. He challenges and encourages the Christian writer, visual artist or composer and their church community, to embrace and be true to this calling with art that is real and compassionate, that sees the true and complex beauty of the world but also its profound brokenness, within the context of a redeeming grace—to not let the world have all the fun with the gifts of creativity that have been bestowed upon us as human beings. And he accomplishes this with an ease and clarity that itself is artful.

JOHN TERPSTRA, award-winning writer and poet; author of several works of nonfiction and poetry, including *In the Company of All: Prayers from Sunday Mornings at St. Cuthbert's*

According to Jesus, his disciples are to be in the world but not of it (John 17:14–16). This does not mean that we are to abandon the planet, or humanity *per se*, but that we are forbidden to participate in the rebellion against God that marks this fallen world. This thoughtful series of essays encourages us to think like Christians and to engage the world around as those who have been transformed by God's grace and now view the world through the lens of God's redemption in Christ. As such, it is a delightful exercise in taking every thought captive to make it obedient to Christ. I highly recommend it!

KIRK WELLUM, principal and professor of systematic theology, biblical studies and pastoral studies at Toronto Baptist Seminary

Jeremy has brought together a diverse collection of his own Christian reflections on "culture and the arts." His many years of teaching English literature and the classics and his own genuine appreciation and discernment of—and his wisdom concerning—works as diverse as *The Pilgrim's Progress* and the *Harry Potter* books, have set him up as an experienced and knowledgeable guide to Christians and others interested in Christian thinking.

MIKE WILKINS, a long-time pastor at West London (Ontario) Alliance Church, and the author of *Glory in the Face*

Reading this book inspired me to praise our Creator God for his artistry, reminded me to take in the details of the created world with wide-eyed wonder, and challenged me to take after my Father by using the creativity he has passed on to me. What a helpful, enjoyable, God-glorifying read! And what a great filter through which to examine my day-to-day world.

BARBARA POSTMA, home educator, freelance writer and author of *Hear My Prayers*

All Things New is what is known as a primer—an introduction to first principles on a subject. That subject is announced in the book's subtitle: Christianity, culture, and the arts. The strength of *All Things New* is threefold. The first is the accuracy of the author's thinking about the subjects he takes up. The second is the comprehensiveness of the book, as every important subject receives treatment. The book's third virtue stems from the original appearance of the chapters in a magazine: the book possesses an admirable moderation, as the author gives us just enough on each subject to be helpful but not so much as to tire us. This carries over to the published sources that the author cites: They are a roll call of some of my own favourite authors, but they are not so numerous as to become pedantic. This is a readable book designed for people who want to understand how Christianity relates to culture and the arts.

LELAND RYKEN, professor emeritus of English at Wheaton College and author and editor of several books including *Realms of Gold* and *The Christian Imagination*

This book functions as both a guide and a model for how we should be engaging culture as Christians. Whether you are fresh to the subject or a seasoned explorer, there is a lot to be gleaned for every reader. *All Things New* is written as a series of very short chapters allowing you plenty of space for pause and reflection. Together they cover a huge range of subjects related to what has traditionally been called 'high culture'; i.e., the arts. We are introduced to the world of paintings, literature, music and film. Jeremy's own passion and love for this shines through, as does his love for Jesus. He writes with the expressed intention that we bring this domain of life under Christ's lordship. Here is a piece of writing that wonderfully combines the Bible and theology with many illustrations from the world of the arts—both old and new. Jeremy has the gift of word-smithing and expressing rather complex ideas with a wonderful perspicuity. *All Things New* deserves a wide readership.

ANDREW FELLOWS, director of Christian Heritage in Cambridge, England, and former chair of L'Abri International

ALL THINGS NEW

Essays on Christianity, culture & the arts

Jeremy W. Johnston

www.joshuapress.com

Published by
Joshua Press Inc., Kitchener, Ontario, Canada
Distributed by
Sola Scriptura Ministries International
www.sola-scriptura.ca

First published 2018
© 2018 Jeremy W. Johnston. All rights reserved. This book may not be reproduced, in whole or in part, without written permission from the publishers.

Cover and book design by Janice Van Eck

Unless otherwise indicated, all Scripture quotations are from The ESV® Bible (The Holy Bible, English Standard Version®), copyright © 2001 by Crossway, a publishing ministry of Good News Publishers. Used by permission. All rights reserved.

The publication of this book was made possible by the generous support of The Ross-Shire Foundation.

Library and Archives Canada Cataloguing in Publication

Johnston, Jeremy W., 1975–, author
    All things new : essays on Christianity, culture & the arts / Jeremy W. Johnston.

Most essays previously published in *Barnabas* magazine.
Includes bibliographical references and indexes.
Issued in print and electronic formats.
ISBN 978-1-894400-90-9 (softcover).—ISBN 978-1-894400-91-6 (HTML).—ISBN 978-1-894400-92-3 (PDF)

    1. Christianity and culture. 2. Christianity and the arts.
I. Title.

BR115.C8J64 2018   261   C2018-903323-1
                                                           C2018-903324-X

To my wife Laurie

> For thy sweet love remembered such wealth brings,
> That then I scorn to change my state with kings.
> —William Shakespeare, *Sonnet 29*

Lights moved along that cross from horn to horn
and from the summit to the base, and as
they met and passed, they sparkled, radiant [...]
   And just as harp and viol, whose many chords
are tempered, taut, produce sweet harmony
although each single note is not distinct,
   so, from the lights that then appeared to me,
out from that cross there spread a melody
that held me rapt, although I could not tell
   what hymn it was. I knew it sang high praise,
since I heard "Rise" and "Conquer," but I was
as one who hears but cannot seize the sense.
   Yet I was so enchanted by the sound
that until then no thing had ever bound
me with such gentle bonds.

—Dante Alighieri, *Paradiso*, Canto XIV, ll. 109–111;
118–129, Allen Mandelbaum, trans.)

Contents

Foreword — xi
Preface—Glorifying God through arts & culture — xv
Acknowledgements—My debt to great thinkers, inspiring mentors & loving supporters — xxi

I. ON ART & CREATIVITY
Reflecting an artistic God — 3
Use your imagination — 7
God's delight in beauty — 11
Art & idolatry — 15
Understanding art — 19
Art of food: Taste & see — 23
Love, empathy & art — 27

II. ON THE ARTIST'S CALL
Created to be creative — 33
Gifted for such a time as this — 37
Art for God's sake — 41
Pursing excellence in art — 45
Don't waste your talent — 49
Helping the church get used to "all things new" — 53

III. ON LITERATURE

Poetry, microwaves, & Big Macs	59
Why we should read fiction	63
Narnia, Harry Potter & *Lord of the Rings*: Are there bad stories?	67
Monsters in the mirror	71
Bunyan's *The Pilgrim's Progress*	75
Shakespeare's world(view)	79
Imagining reality in *Hamlet*	83
Jane Austen: Small joys & simple pleasures	87

IV. ON MUSIC

Reforming music: Bach & Luther	93
J.S. Bach: "Do all to the glory of God"	97
Handel's masterpiece	101

V. ON CINEMA

Pitching your tents	107
A case for movie-making	111

VI. ON FAITH & CULTURE

Reforming art	117
Darwin & the shrivelling of our artistic "soul"	121
What about nudity in art?	125
Bridging old & new traditions	131
The beautiful cross	135

For further reading	139
Scripture index	141
Index	143
About the author	147

Foreword

As a designer and editor, culture and the arts have been my lifeblood. As both a practitioner and appreciator, I have wrestled with how to maintain and present a Christian worldview as I navigate this complex world. Back in the early 90s, I found it difficult to find resources to help think through some of the things I was seeing and experiencing in the art and publishing world. I came across *The Creative Gift: The Arts and the Christian Life* by H.R. Rookmaaker and was greatly helped at the time. He writes,

> Art needs no justification. It is meaningful in itself, not only as an evangelistic tool, or to serve a practical purpose, or to be didactic. Art must be free: free from politics…traditions of the past…the judgement of the future…our economic and social needs. Art cannot be turned into a mere function of any of these without losing its indispensable place in human life. After all, Christ died in order to restore our humanity, and to give meaning back to God's creation. Not only is evangelism Christian, but *all of life is Christian*, unless we would make Christ very small.[1]

---

[1] H.R. Rookmaaker, *The Creative Gift: The Arts and the Christian Life* (Leicester: Inter-Varsity Press, 1981), 112. Emphasis added.

Elsewhere, Rookmaaker states,

We cannot make art apart from the time in which we live. We must know what is going on, and understand our environment if we want to achieve anything of relevance to our times. We must also know the spirit of our times in order to know where it is wrong and should be challenged and fought. We may look for inspiration to the arts of the past—but we may never be slaves of the past.... God, in placing us in another period, has given us our own calling: to be 'salting salt' today, to hunger and thirst for righteousness in the here and now.[2]

Seeing the vital place of art and culture in the world means that Christians can bring a unique, redemptive hope to this area of society. Our works—whether of composition, poetry, fiction, painting, design, photography, video, etc.—as children of a loving Father, will reflect him as we seek the Spirit's power to use our gifts for his glory. That doesn't mean that we only work in "sacred" areas, but "all of life is Christian," as Rookmaaker reminds us. *Wherever* we use our talents—artistic or otherwise—on all kinds of topics and areas, we are to reflect a worldview that has been transformed—liberated—by the gospel of Jesus Christ. Now that's exciting!

When we started *Barnabas* ten years ago, as editor I knew I wanted to see columns that would engage readers on both culture and the arts. Finding Jeremy Johnston was definitely a gift from God, and he has proved to be an able, engaged and insightful columnist. In our frenzied society, there can seem little time for thoughtful reflection on key issues, and I'm thankful Jeremy does just that: helps us slow down and think through our engagement with the arts, challenges us to think deeper about our

---

[2] H.R. Rookmaaker, *Modern Art and the Death of a Culture* (Wheaton: Crossway, 1994), 245.

callings and encourages healthy appreciation and critique of culture and the arts, even as they reflect our creative God. Jeremy reminds us often of the *value* of imagination, the *enrichment* creativity brings to all of society and the *delight* the arts bring to daily life. I couldn't agree more.

It is a real joy to see the fruits of those many deadlines now being reborn in a new format—a collection of essays—and more widely available to a fresh audience. I hope many will benefit from and be encouraged by Jeremy's writings as they cultivate artistic pursuits themselves or desire to be better appreciators and supporters of those who are engaged in the arts today.

Janice Van Eck
Editor & art director, *Barnabas*
May 23, 2018

Preface—Glorifying God through arts & culture

> Let every good and true Christian understand that wherever truth may be found, it belongs to his Master.
> —Augustine, *On Christian Doctrine*, II.18

> Shall we deem anything to be noble and praiseworthy, without tracing it to the hand of God? Far from us be such ingratitude; an ingratitude not chargeable even on heathen poets, who acknowledge that philosophy and laws, and all useful arts, were the inventions of the gods.
> —John Calvin, *Institutes of the Christian Religion*

Why publish a collection of essays on Christianity, culture and the arts? The apostle Paul exhorts us to think about "whatever is true, whatever is honourable, whatever is just, whatever is pure, whatever is lovely, whatever is commendable" (Philippians 4:8). The world of the arts and culture can be "lovely" and "commendable," but is this what Paul meant? Is it a waste of time to think about the arts and culture of this world? Shouldn't we be thinking about the world to come, good doctrine or advancing the gospel of Christ? Paul says, "If there is any excellence, if there is anything worthy of praise, think about these things" (Philippians 4:8). Is there "any excellence" beyond the church walls that is worth thinking about? Can truth be found in art and culture produced outside Christian communities? The answer to both these questions is yes.

ALL THINGS UNDER THE LORDSHIP OF CHRIST

In *On Christian Doctrine*, Augustine writes that "wherever truth may be found, it belongs to his Master!"[1] All truth is God's truth. The apostle Paul illustrates the point by harkening Athenians to see glimmers of the truth even in their own altar to the unknown god on Mars Hill (see Acts 17:16–34). Paul knew that the Athenian unbelievers had, in their heart of hearts, an awareness of the supreme living God (Romans 1:18–21), so he used this truth hidden among their altars and poets to reveal the truth of God to them.

Christians have a tendency to divide *secular* and *sacred* concerns; in fact, *everything* belongs to the Lord. "All that is in the heavens and in the earth is yours," writes the author of Chronicles. "Yours is the kingdom, O Lord and you are exalted as head above all" (1 Chronicles 29:11). All aspects of creation—"all that is in the heavens and in the earth"—belong to God.

The twentieth-century apologist, Francis Schaeffer, frequently points out that "true spirituality covers all of reality." For him, this supremacy of Christ's lordship was no less significant in the world of arts and culture. He emphasizes this point in his book *Art and the Bible*: "If Christianity is really true, then it involves the whole man, including his *intellect* and *creativeness*."[2] The gospel of Jesus Christ transforms our actions, our hearts and our desires. However, the gospel transforms our intellectual and creative faculties as well. Schaeffer goes on to say, "Christianity is not just 'dogmatically' true or 'doctrinally' true. Rather, it is true to what is there, true in the whole area of the whole man in all of life."

---

[1] Augustine, *On Christian Doctrine*, II.18.28.
[2] Francis A. Schaeffer, *Art and the Bible* (Downers Grove: InterVarsity Press, 2006), 16.

CULTURE APPRECIATORS

This doesn't mean that all art and all culture are good or worthy of our time. Biblical discretion and Spirit-led discernment are still needed. As Christians, however, we can confidently approach the art and culture of our world because it is under the dominion of Christ. We can appreciate the truth, goodness and beauty that can be found and benefit from it for God's glory and our enjoyment. In his excellent book on the literary achievements of the classical Greco-Roman world, Peter J. Leithart compares Christians gleaning truth and beauty from "pagan" sources to the Israelites plundering Egypt's gold during the Exodus. He writes,

> It is fully within the rights of Christians, to whom, in Christ, belong "all things" (1 Corinthians 3:21–23), to plunder these stories and make what use of them we can. Because some treasures of Athens, purged with fire, may, like the gold of Egypt, finally adorn Jerusalem.[3]

Like the "plundered" gold from Egypt, Christians are able to gain wisdom and enjoy much beauty when taking in and engaging with the creative and cultural achievements of humanity. We already do this in other areas of life, such as our appreciation and use of fine clothing, attractive houses, innovative technology and good food. Very few people insist on only wearing the clothes made by Christians or only eating food prepared by members of the church. Good stories, like good dinners, can be enjoyed regardless of who made them; fine artwork, like a well-tailored suit or dress, can bring us much joy and delight whether made by a believer or unbeliever. Our delight in the creative faculties of human beings ultimately brings glory to the One who made humanity in his image. God is a creative being who endowed men and women—his imagebearers—with an ability and desire to create beauty and culture.

---

[3] Peter J. Leithart, *Heroes of the City of Man: A Christian Guide to Select Ancient Literature* (Moscow: Canon Press, 1999), 38.

CULTURE-REDEEMERS

A challenge to the idea that Christians should enjoy arts and culture may be that so much of it—both inside and outside the church—is terrible. Nowhere is this more evident than in recent decades, especially within the Western world of arts and culture, where there have been few "excellent things" to think on or to appreciate. As Christians living in the twenty-first century, we are feeling the all-encompassing effect of the last 100 years of bizarre cultural achievements lacking truth, beauty and goodness, which is borne out of the prevailing worldviews of despairing modernism, disillusioned postmodernism and discordant post-postmodernism. Art galleries feel like distant places, containing works of art that seem to have no relation to the things that really matter in life. Good stories have either been supplanted by pessimistic tales and shallow escapism, or they have been spirited away by the morticians of academia to be dissected rather than digested. The beautiful legacy of orchestral and choral music is appreciated by shrinking audiences made up of aging listeners and a handful of music aficionados. Culture itself has been expropriated by consumer and corporate interests to be repackaged and rebranded for quick sales and easy profit. Film, television and pornography have taken us back to gladiatorial-like arenas, where degrading shock and dehumanizing horror encompass the paltry and unsatisfying range of amusement and entertainment.

Devoid of truth, beauty and goodness, and with so little to appreciate, celebrate or enjoy, shouldn't Christians just avoid the whole realm of arts and culture, which seems so useless and so corrupt?

Gene Edward Veith, Jr. writes,

> That the arts can be corrupt does not mean that Christians should abandon them. On the contrary, the corruption of

the arts means that Christians dare not abandon them any longer. Art—like all things human—needs to be redeemed.[4]

Christians are called to be "salt and light" (Matthew 5:13–16); there is work to be done in redeeming all aspects of this world—social, religious, political, economic, scientific, medical, educational—so also the area of arts and culture. This doesn't mean that we are called to create a Christian kingdom or political state this side of glory. It does mean, however, that Christians—wherever God has placed them—are to glorify God by bringing to bear biblical truth, God-fearing wisdom and Christian mercy, grace and love. This is because the gospel of Jesus Christ is more than a "call to the unsaved" to be saved: the gospel is about *total lives* being *totally transformed*. The gospel calls us to show how faith redeems not only our spiritual lives but all aspects of our entire being—how we think, what we enjoy, why we create, what we believe, where we live and what we do. Edith Schaeffer, the co-founder of L'Abri, writes, "The whole person is involved in being a Christian. The whole life is involved in living in contact with God."[5] Not just parts of our lives, but *all* of our lives—and this includes the arts and culture that surround us.

CULTURE-MAKERS

Being culture-redeemers is not the only call for Christians; we are also called, as human beings, to be makers of culture. Timothy Keller argues that God's commission to Adam and Eve in the Garden of Eden—and to Christians today—is a call to be creators of culture.[6] God placed the first human beings in a garden not a wilderness. A garden is something that requires design, hard work and care—that is, cultivation. Culture, like a

---

[4] Gene Edward Veith, Jr., *State of the Arts: From Bezalel to Mapplethorpe* (Wheaton: Crossway, 1991), xvi.
[5] Edith Schaeffer, *L'Abri* (Wheaton: Crossway, 1992), 157.
[6] See, for example, chapter 3 of Timothy Keller, *Every Good Endeavor: Connecting Your Work to God's Work* (New York: Riverhead Books, 2012).

garden, requires cultivators. We were made to be makers; we were called to be creators. Keller writes about the *undeveloped potential* of God's creation: "The pattern of all work...is creative and assertive. It is rearranging the raw material of God's creation in such a way that it helps the world in general, and people in particular, thrive and flourish."[7]

God's commission to Adam and Eve to "fill the earth" means both building families and building civilizations (Genesis 1:28). Humanity is still called to both procreation and culture creation. This involves a range of things that Christians can and *must* have a hand in developing, from political structures and works of civil engineering to arts, literature and music. Christians, alongside all human beings, need to be *appreciators* of art and culture. But, Christians also need to be culture-*makers* and culture-*redeemers*, filling the earth with new, created things for the glory of the supreme Creator.

Soli Deo gloria!

Jeremy W. Johnston
Hamilton, ON

---

[7] Keller, *Every Good Endeavor*, 47.

Acknowledgements
—My debt to great thinkers, inspiring mentors & loving supporters

As iron sharpens iron, so one man sharpens another.
—Proverbs 27:17

I have laboured to give credit where credit is due; however, such is the impact of great teachers that it can be difficult to differentiate between their influence and one's own original thoughts. Therefore, I must acknowledge the colossal impact of my teachers-in-print who have shaped my thinking and illuminated my understanding of the arts: Peter J. Leithart, Leland Ryken, Gene Edward Veith, Jr., Philip Ryken, Douglas Wilson, R.C. Sproul, John Piper, Timothy Keller, Jerram Barrs, Dorothy Sayers, Flannery O'Connor, Francis Schaeffer, G.K. Chesterton, J.R.R. Tolkien and, most of all, I am especially indebted to the writings of C.S. Lewis. These writers and thinkers have influenced me so much on this subject that I hardly know where their influence ends and my ideas begin.

In appreciation of my mentors-in-the-flesh, who have taught me much about faith and the arts, I must first acknowledge two dear brothers in Christ who have both gone home to glory this year. The first is my friend and former pastor, Mike Wilkins. Over the last twenty years I knew him, Mike taught me both in "word and deed" how the gospel impacts all areas of life, from the heart and mind, to family, work and the broader realm of arts and culture. Another mentor who helped me bridge faith with arts, music and literature is Bryan Wylie, master teacher and my predecessor teaching English and Latin at Hillfield Strathallan College in Hamilton, Ontario. Right up to a few months before "shuffling off this mortal coil," he continued to give lectures on the subject of "the Christian and the arts" at Philpott Memorial Church and other local community venues in Hamilton.

Another mentor-in-the-flesh is my former student, Gordon Vanderwoude, who is also a talented musician, teacher and very dear friend. He provided me with guidance and insight in the areas of music and film. As a writer, I am grateful to Janice Van Eck, editor of *Barnabas*. I am thankful for her support for my writing as well as her efficiency in editing and refining my pieces to make them readable and presentable to real audiences. Her encouragement and prodding also helped to convince me that I am a *bona fide* writer, and writing is something I *should* do for the glory of God. For this particular book project, I want to thank her for her behind-the-scenes labours editing and designing the layout and her invaluable help to bring this collection of essays into publishable form. Through her excellent craftsmanship and artistry she brings glory to the One who made her "for such a time as this." I am also very thankful for Michael Haykin and Heinz Dschankilic of Joshua Press for their interest in publishing this book and for their efforts bringing it to press. Kudos must be given to my friend and mentor, Mark Hudson, coordinator of Sovereign Grace Fellowship of Canada, who, along with Janice, originally provided me with the opportunity to write a regular column on the arts for *Barnabas* magazine. Without the venue (and the deadlines), I would have very little to show in this already slim volume!

Another key supporter of this book project is my friend and colleague, Melissa Poremba; I am tremendously grateful for her thorough scrutinizing of this manuscript as one of my main copyeditors. She has gone above and beyond the call of duty, helping to make this book as clear and readable as possible. I thank her for her wise advice and discerning eye as a reader. I also thank her for the countless hours poring over this manuscript multiple times, for researching the finer points of *Chicago Style* citations and for offering up dozens of insightful suggestions for improving the book. I have endeavoured to amend all the errors, incongruities and weaknesses she diligently uncovered; if mistakes still remain, then the fault is entirely my own.

I am indebted to my home church, Pilgrim Baptist Fellowship, for allowing me to work out my thoughts on faith and the arts during many devotionals, Christian education classes and sermons on the subject over the past ten years. Thank-you, especially, to Paul McCallum who encouraged me to minister to the church through the examination of the arts; his consistent feedback, appreciation and frequent requests for these sorts of unusual and unconventional Bible lessons have been the catalyst for much of what you see here in this volume. I also cherish his brotherly love and friendship. Without a doubt, he has been my "Jack" and I aspire to be his "Tollers"—that is, kindred spirits and brothers-in-arms for the good and glorious gospel. "Oil and perfume make the heart glad, and the sweetness of a friend comes from his earnest counsel" (Proverbs 27:9).

My parents have been an unending support of me and my writing; I thank God for them. They encouraged me as I spent hours of my youth plunking away on typewriters crafting silly stories that (thankfully) are lost to posterity. I especially thank my mother—a writer herself—for instilling in me a love of words and wordsmithing. My siblings—Melissa Kirkpatrick and Jeff Johnston—have likewise been stalwart supporters in the realms of faith, family, the arts and education, and they have always encouraged me to use the gifts God has given me for his glory and the building up of the church.

I would like to offer special thanks to my own dear family:

first, my children—Joseph, Nate, Katie and Abby, who are gifts from my "Father of lights"—I am grateful for their admiration and love, though I often feel unworthy of both. To my beloved wife, Laurie, I want to express my gratitude for over twenty years of love and devotion both to me and to our family; she faithfully serves in innumerable ways, but I am most thankful for the beauty she brings to my life and to the lives of others: one such way is her unceasing labour making our home and gardens inviting, cozy and aesthetically pleasing—what the Dutch call *gezellig*. I also want to thank her for being my first test audience and for enabling me to retreat to my study to read and to write. While I dabble in the world of writing and the arts, her respect and love have been inspiring and comforting to me; it is to her that I have dedicated this volume of essays.

Lastly, to Christ, in whom I live and breathe and have my being.... My finite gratitude cannot do justice to him who is the fount of all that is good and lovely. To him be glory, forever and ever! Amen!

I

ON ART & CREATIVITY

ON ART & CREATIVITY
Reflecting an artistic God

This essay considers the example of two artists named in the Bible—Bezalel and Oholiab—in order to ascertain why art and beauty matter to God and why art and beauty should matter to us.[1]

Bezalel and Oholiab are little known Bible characters, and yet they are significant.[2] They are significant because they are the first people in the recorded biblical narrative to be inspired by the Holy Spirit.[3] They are also significant because they are artists. God called and enabled these two men to craft the various artwork and decorations for worship in the Tabernacle (Exodus 31:1–11). Although this was a unique and specific call for these artists, there is much we can learn from their example.

God inspired Bezalel and Oholiab to create works of art to aid in worship. Many of the objects had divinely articulated

---

[1] Originally published in *Barnabas*, Vol. 3, No. 1 (Winter 2011): 11.
[2] I am indebted to Gene Edward Veith, Jr. and Philip Graham Ryken for drawing my attention to these Bible characters, so easily overlooked in the grand narrative of Exodus; see Gene Edward Veith, Jr., *State of the Arts: From Bezalel to Mapplethorpe* (Wheaton: Crossway, 1991) and Philip Graham Ryken, *Art for God's Sake: A Call to Recover the Arts* (New Jersey: P&R Publishing, 2006).
[3] Veith, Jr., *State of the Arts*, 108.

specifications. But God also gave Bezalel artistic ability in order to "devise artistic designs" (Exodus 31:4). God gave Bezalel room for creativity. Artists are called to take old truths and present them in new, fresh and engaging ways. Sometimes people become complacent with truth. Art should awaken viewers, listeners and readers anew to the realities of ancient truth. *Creativity matters.*

God, the supreme artist, bestows artistic skills, talents and vision upon human beings. Ultimately, the glory and praise should always go to him. However, what an artist does with his or her talents is also important. The Bible states that Bezalel's and Oholiab's artistic abilities were gifts from God, but it also states that they were "able men"—men who had honed and practiced their skills. God uses skilled and practiced artists for his purposes. *Proficiency and practice matter.*

God manifested himself and his truth through the representational art created by Bezalel and Oholiab. But not everything in art is necessarily symbolic, nor does it need to be. The priests' garments, for example, were decorated with blue pomegranates (Exodus 28:33). Why pomegranates and why blue? There may be a theological purpose that a keen scholar may someday discern, but sometimes the purpose of art is simply to *delight*. As we delight in beauty our attention is drawn to God, who is, according to Wayne Grudem, "the sum of all desirable qualities."[4] Beauty exists only because God exists as the Beautiful One. And, beauty's fundamental function is to delight. *Beauty matters.*

Why does God use art at all? The answer to that question is also the answer to why we use art in worship today. Instead of reciting the *1689 Baptist Confession of Faith* or reading portions from Wayne Grudem's *Systematic Theology* (as excellent as these resources are), we sing hymns, psalms and poems, often set to beautiful and stirring music. Art speaks to our emotions as well

---

[4] Wayne Grudem, *Systematic Theology: An Introduction to Biblical Doctrine* (Leicester: Inter-Varsity, 1994), 219.

as to our minds; it moves us holistically. Art makes truth accessible to us. Like the inspired artists who built the Tabernacle, individuals were also inspired by God to pen the Bible in "literary form" using artful and poetic devices.[5] A significant portion of the Scriptures takes the form of artistic storytelling and poetry. God intentionally uses art to communicate his truth to his people. *Art matters.*

God gave Bezalel ability and skill in "every craft" (Exodus 31:5). God is interested in all kinds of art. Whether you are an artist who paints, composes, sculpts, designs, writes or sings, God has given you your ability; God can use your art for his glory and his purposes. Pray that he will grant you the wisdom to use it well. "Whatever you do, do all to the glory of God" (1 Corinthians 10:31).

---

[5] See, for example, Leland Ryken and Philip Graham Ryken, eds., *The Literary Study Bible, English Standard Version* (Wheaton: Crossway Bibles, 2007).

ON ART & CREATIVITY
Use your imagination

Humanity is made in the image of God; among the attributes passed on to humanity is creativity. Every person possesses the ability—albeit in varying degrees—to imagine like the divine Creator. This essay makes a case for Christians to develop and use their imaginations to not only be creative but also to assist finite minds in comprehending the mystery of the gospel and aid us in our growing understanding of the infinite God. Like all gifts given to us by God, we need to be stewards, faithfully honing and exercising our imagination for his glory and our benefit. This is achieved not only by taking in creative works, but also by producing new creative works.[1]

Listening to John Lennon's 1971 song, "Imagine," causes most people to liken "imagination" with mere "wishful thinking." But in truth, "imagination" is an aspect of the divine mind, which he gives to humanity to help us understand true reality, including his own character and his dealings with the world. In Scripture, God describes himself using imaginative language—what theologians call analogous language; he is depicted as a Father, King, Brother,

---

[1] Originally published in *Barnabas*, Vol. 1, No. 3 (Fall 2009): 10.

Husband, Lover and Friend, but he is not *literally* any of these things. He is Spirit and does not have a body, yet he is described as having a face, ears, eyes, nostrils, mouth, hands, arms, fingers, shoulders, back and feet; he sits, stands, marches, rides, shoots arrows and has a voice like thunder. Through metaphor and poetic imagery—understood by a sanctified imagination—finite minds begin to comprehend their infinite and unfathomable Creator. Through imaginative means, God reveals himself to us.

Imagination also helps us to understand the full spectrum of God's world—both the material and the nonmaterial aspects of creation. The created universe is more than molecules and cells, chemical reactions and calculations. Imagination aids our ability to know and appreciate the intangible aspects of reality: aspects like love, courage, friendship, beauty, sacrifice, honour, glory and even "angels and principalities." By exercising a sanctified imagination, Christians can counter the narrowing perspectives of our culture's scientific worldview, a worldview that claims "what is nonmaterial is immaterial."

A sanctified imagination also enables Christians to understand the mysteries of the gospel, mysteries that are often spoken of poetically. The Gospels give countless examples where listeners of Jesus misunderstood the message because of narrow and pragmatic mindsets. For example, when Jesus warned of the "leaven of the Pharisees," the disciples asked, "Where's the bread?" (Matthew 16:5–7). Too often we skim over word pictures painted by Jesus without imagining the full impact of what the Word is conveying. The Golden Rule, "Love your neighbour as yourself," is given poetically. In order to love our neighbour, we must imagine we are walking in his or her shoes. We must also imagine what Christ would do in our situation. For example, husbands are to love their wives the way Christ loves the church. In other words, husbands need to *imagine* what that sort of love looks like in their marriages and then do it.

Lastly, we are to use our imaginations to communicate God's glory anew. Francis Schaeffer writes, "The Christian is the one whose imagination should fly beyond the stars."[2] God is too wonderful to be praised with worn out clichés; the imagination is needed to communicate the glory of God to each new generation and culture. In his essay "God is not boring," John Piper writes,

> Imagination is like a muscle. It grows stronger when you flex it. Imagination is also contagious. So I suggest that you hang out with people (mainly dead poets) who are full of imagination. Then labour to say an old truth in awakening ways. God is worthy. "Oh sing to the Lord a new song"—or picture, or poem, or figure of speech.[3]

Let us be diligent in fostering sanctified imaginations, in order to know God, to know reality and to make him known in the world, here and now. Read a poem, write a poem, drain the ocean dry and fill the sky...imagine.

---

[2] Francis A. Schaeffer, *Art and the Bible* (Downers Grove: InterVarsity Press, 2006), 91.
[3] John Piper, "God Is Not Boring," *Desiring God*, February 26, 2003, www.desiringgod.org.

ON ART & CREATIVITY
God's delight in beauty

Is beauty in the eye of the beholder? Is beauty only skin deep? This essay examines the counter-cultural and biblical view of beauty and the importance God places on it as a means of bringing glory to himself and delighting his people. Although many evangelical Christians have resisted postmodernism in the areas of theology and ethics, the area of beauty seems to have been surrendered to the relativistic spirit of the age.[1]

Truth. Goodness. Beauty. These three words formed the medieval church's vision of God, the ultimate standard for truth, goodness and beauty. Today, our postmodern culture[2] has relegated these three pivotal ideas to the realm of relativity. Everything, it is said, is relative to the perspective of the individual. You may

---

[1] Originally published in *Barnabas*, Vol. 3, No. 3 (Summer 2011): 11.

[2] Postmodernism is essentially about deconstructing the "imposed meaning" of cultural, social, traditional and institutional constructs; the goal is to "liberate" humanity to pursue individual and personalized meaning. For example, when debating "universal truth," a common postmodern rebuttal is, "What is true for you is true for you, but what is true for me is true for me." For an excellent discussion of "postmodernity," see Chapter 9 of James W. Sire, *The Universe Next Door: A Basic Worldview Catalog* (Downers Grove: InterVarsity Press, 2004).

have heard these statements rolling off the lips of coworkers, friends or family members: "What is true for you is not necessarily true for me..." or "Good is whatever *you want* it to be or whatever *feels right* to you." The church is well-trained to reject this view of truth and goodness. Beauty, however, is a concept that Christians have neglected. "Beauty is in the eye of the beholder"—is a phrase many people use, Christians and non-Christians alike. Truth or goodness is certainly not "in the eye of the beholder"—but what about beauty?

To God, beauty is more than a pleasant distraction or digression from serious business. In decreeing the design of the Temple, God incorporates elements that have no function other than beauty (1 Chronicles 28:11–12; 2 Chronicles 3:6–10, 16–17). God integrates beauty into his place of worship because beauty declares his glory. Beauty is also important in worship because it causes God's people to delight in him, the ultimate standard of beauty.

In his book *Art and the Bible*, Francis Schaeffer criticized the proliferation of "ugliness in evangelical church buildings."[3] This is because modern Christianity has adopted the world's view of beauty. Only practicality and function seem to matter. But God created a world which contains stunning beauty, beauty that has no function other than for God's delight and ours. Gazing upon a sunset is strikingly sublime...enrapturing...but functionless in the pragmatic sense. When God punctuates his promise to Noah by creating the rainbow, he makes it beautiful but it serves no functional purpose other than a reminder of God's promises (Genesis 9:8–17). During Creation, God created a garden with trees bearing food—which is very useful in a practical sense—but we are told he also made the fruit "pleasing to the eye" (Genesis 2:9)—beautiful! Beauty matters to God.

To emphasize the point, the Bible uses the word "beauty" (or its derivatives) over seventy times throughout the Scriptures.

---

[3] Francis A. Schaeffer, *Art and the Bible* (Downers Grove: InterVarcity Press, 2006), 26.

Francis Schaeffer writes, "Come with me to the Alps and look at the snow covered mountains. There can be no question. God is interested in beauty. God made people to be beautiful. And beauty has a place in the worship of God."[4]

Ultimately beauty is a spiritual concept; Christ's love for the church is a beautiful thing. Conversion of lost souls is beautiful. "How beautiful are the feet of those who bring good news," writes the apostle Paul (Romans 10:15; see Isaiah 52:7). But beauty is not limited to spiritual things only. Daisies are beautiful. Waterfalls, mossy stones, majestic trees are beautiful. Sleeping babies are beautiful. Nor is beauty limited to the natural world either. Beauty is the business of art. Music can be beautiful. Sculpture can be beautiful. Hymns can be beautiful. Architecture can be beautiful. Fashion can be beautiful.

As Christians, we need to develop a biblical and God-glorifying appreciation of beauty—a Christian aesthetic. We should ask, How can we add more beauty to our lives, our homes and our churches? In his essay, "The Aesthetic Poverty of Evangelicalism" Clyde Kilby writes, "Our excuse for our aesthetic failure has often been that we must be about the Lord's business, the assumption being that the Lord's business is never aesthetic."[5] But if God is truly concerned about beauty, then why aren't we?

---

[4] Schaeffer, *Art and the Bible*, 26.
[5] Clyde S. Kilby, "The Aesthetic Poverty of Evangelicalism," in *The Christian Imagination: The Practice of Faith in Literature and Writing*, ed. Leland Ryken (Colorado Springs: Shaw Books, 2005), 278.

ON ART & CREATIVITY
Art & idolatry

This essay considers how art has been used historically within Christianity and the Bible; at times, art is a helpful aid to worship and at other times it can be a distraction. Even though art can be a very important part of worship, if it (or anything else) distracts us from the living God, it is an idol and should be cast away.[1]

Art is powerful. The medieval church used and misused it, Reformers cautioned about it and sometimes destroyed it and the Bible frequently warns against the abuse of it, specifically in the form of idol worship. Today, idolatry can come in many forms: careers, family, possessions—anything that usurps God's rightful place in our lives. Timothy Keller defines idolatry simply as "turning a good thing into an ultimate thing."[2] Idolatry, however, is most seductive and most powerful when it comes in the form of art.

How the church uses art, then, is an important consideration. The early church and the medieval church produced a host of

---
[1] Originally published in *Barnabas*, Vol. 4, No. 1 (Winter 2012): 7.
[2] Timothy Keller, *Every Good Endeavor: Connecting Your Work to God's Work* (New York: Riverhead Books, 2012), 128

amazing paintings, mosaics, stained glass, frescoes, statues, carvings and other forms of stunning and beautiful art. Unfortunately, some of this art portrayed unbiblical concepts and errors in doctrine. The end result was ungodly superstition surrounding many works of art. With the advent of the Reformation, Christians debated what to do with art inside the church. The Reformers' main concern regarding visual art was the potential it had to distract worshippers from the truth of God, whether by conveying false messages or supplanting the written Word as central to worship.

But not all Reformers were iconoclasts, destroying works of art inside (and sometimes outside) the church. While taking refuge at Wartburg castle, Martin Luther learned that zealous Reformers were destroying stained-glass windows, furniture and other forms of art in the churches of Wittenburg. Despite the risk to his own life, Luther returned to Wittenburg to stop the destruction of the artwork. Certainly, Luther supported the removal of heretical art, such as images depicting Mary in a redemptive role or images of saints and extra-biblical events and legends. But Luther also supported and encouraged the use of art, especially music, in worship. For Luther, the main concern was not necessarily the *form* of art, but rather its *purpose*: What did the art communicate to worshippers?

The Bible addresses the use of art in worship in a "tale of two artists" recorded in Exodus. In chapter 31, we read that God calls the artist Bezalel to construct works of art for use in worship. The art pieces were intended to convey spiritual meaning to worshippers. In the very next chapter (Exodus 32) we read of another "gifted artist"—Aaron—who fashioned out of gold a work of art which was also intended to convey meaning.[3] The difference between the two was that Bezalel's works pointed worshippers to God and his plan for salvation, whereas Aaron's

---

[3] Gene Edward Veith, Jr., *State of the Arts: From Bezalel to Mapplethorpe* (Wheaton: Crossway, 1991), 133.

work pointed worshippers to itself, an idol, and ultimately to humanity's self-indulgence. Like many of the icons and idols created during the Middle Ages, Aaron's golden calf was palatable and controllable; the artwork could be used to pacify and gratify the worshippers. In contrast, the living God—to whom Bezalel's artwork pointed—was terrifying and supreme.

Christians today differ dramatically on what to do with art inside the church. Should there be artwork? What kinds or styles are appropriate? What subjects should art depict? The issue in Exodus is not whether Aaron or Bezalel used art in worship, or what style they used (the Bible gives no preference to certain designs), or what they depicted with their art (for both Aaron and Bezalel fashioned bovine sculptures)...*the issue is in the message.* Does the art exalt biblical truth or degrade and convolute it? Does the artwork point us to the living God or distract us from him? One is an aid to worship; the other becomes an idol.

ON ART & CREATIVITY
Understanding art

This essay considers the challenges faced by most people when trying to appreciate the often weird and wacky world of fine art; if art really matters, then how can we best enjoy and understand it?[1]

For most families, a top ten list of "fun family outings" rarely includes a trip to the art gallery. Fine art is foreign to us, and art exhibitions can seem confusing and even pointless. Our confusion is further compounded when we ask, "What does this painting mean?" only to hear a cryptic response from the curator: "Don't you see? The question is the meaning...." Huh? Suddenly, stomachs start growling and families head to the food court; there they partake of a more accessible form of art—the culinary arts (i.e., an overpriced lunch).

To begin making sense of all those rooms filled with paintings and sculptures, it is helpful to understand how art works. Generally speaking, there are three different kinds of fine art: abstract art, representational art and symbolic art.[2] We may prefer one

---

[1] Originally published in *Barnabas*, Vol. 4, No. 3 (Summer 2012): 11.
[2] Gene Edward Veith, Jr., *State of the Arts: From Bezalel to Mapplethorpe* (Wheaton: Crossway, 1991), 115.

kind of art over another, but it is important to note that all three categories have merit and have been used by God and his church over the centuries.

The first kind of art, *abstract art*, is simply *pure* design; it represents nothing "tangible" outside of itself. Modern abstract art, like Jackson Pollack's splatter paintings, often draws from an impoverished worldview. This sort of abstract art venerates meaninglessness, chaos and futility, much to the chagrin of both Christians and uninitiated art enthusiasts. But abstract art can also be beautiful, like the design on a Persian rug, the decorative elements on an illuminated medieval manuscript, the embroidery on a dress, or even the window designs of a modern church building. For example, on the Ark of the Covenant, the priestly garments, the Tabernacle linen and Tabernacle furnishings described in Exodus, many of the artistic features were abstract, reflecting the beauty of design.[3] Gene Edward Veith, Jr. also notes that abstract art can convey "abstractions" such as power, order, beauty or glory.[4] It is easy to "write off" abstract art as pointless; but with careful deliberation, there is often more than meets the eye.

Representational art, on the other hand, attempts to convey literal subjects—items such as the pomegranates, almond blossoms and lilies in Solomon's Temple or the bulls supporting the bronze laver of the Tabernacle. Representational art can also portray supernatural beings like the cherubim. This is the kind of art most people "get" because it literally represents something in the universe. It is, of course, impossible to create representational art depicting God, for art, even in all of its grandeur and beauty, cannot contain the infinite Creator (1 Kings 8:27–30).

The third type of art is symbolic, which uses concrete elements to signify something else. Symbolism, in both fine art and literary art, has often been used to convey attributes and aspects

---

[3] See Exodus 25–28; see also the description of Solomon's Temple in 2 Chronicles 3–4.
[4] Veith, Jr., *State of the Arts*, 117.

of God. The Lion of Judah, for example, symbolizes the strength of Christ, whereas the Lamb of God symbolizes the sacrifice of Christ. Neither symbol is "representational" of Christ, but they symbolize his *qualities*. Because fine art is a visual medium, symbols are a powerful and necessary vehicle for conveying meaning. Sometimes the symbols are not easy to understand. Dorothy Sayers observes that symbols "appeal to the imagination and to the intellect. Interpreting a symbol demands more than finding a one-to-one literal correspondence; it demands and offers a meditative process."[5] This means that it will take time to begin to understand what an artist is trying to accomplish with his or her work.

So, the next time you are in the art gallery, take a lesson from the culinary arts: like good food, fine art should not be taken in quickly.... Enjoy, savour and ruminate...and, pack a lunch.

---

[5] Dorothy L. Sayers, "Introduction" in *The Comedy of Dante Alighieri: Hell*, trans. Dorothy L. Sayers (London: Penguin, 2005), 12.

ON ART & CREATIVITY
Art of food: Taste & see

This essay examines the importance of food not only as a metaphor used throughout the Bible, but also as a means of glorifying our Creator. By our enjoyment of this life-sustaining gift of God, we bring glory to the One who created good food and created humanity with the ability to delight in making and eating it![1]

The Bible has a lot to say about food. There are warnings against gluttony and over-indulgence (Proverbs 23:20–21; Philippians 3:19). But there are also many positive references to food and feasting. In the Old Testament, feasting was linked with marriages (Genesis 29:22; Judges 14:17), hospitality (Genesis 19:3; 26:30), special occasions (1 Kings 8:65; Esther 1:3; Daniel 5:1) as well as the many festivals instituted after the Exodus. The Promised Land is also described as "a land flowing with milk and honey" (Exodus 3:8).

In The New Testament, food continues to be important: one of the key sacraments instituted for the church is the Lord's Supper. Jesus also spent much of his earthly ministry eating and

---

[1] Originally published in *Barnabas*, Vol. 7, No. 2 (Spring 2015): 22.

feasting; he also refers to himself as the "bread of life" (John 6:35, 48) and the Bible itself is often described as spiritual food (Deuteronomy 8:3; 1 Peter 2:2; Hebrews 5:11-14; 1 Corinthians 10:3). To feast on the Word provides both spiritual nourishment and spiritual enjoyment: the psalmist writes, "How sweet are your words to my taste, sweeter than honey to my mouth!" (Psalm 119:103). Heaven is also compared to a wedding spread at an eternal banqueting table (Isaiah 25:6; Matthew 22:2; Revelation 19:7-9). Clearly there is a right way to enjoy food.

Our enjoyment of food teaches us to delight in the spiritual nourishment God provides. Our daily dependence on food also teaches us that we need to feast daily on the Word and on the person of Jesus Christ. Food, however, is more than a metaphor for spiritual blessings, and it is more than physical fuel for our survival. God intends for us to enjoy food this side of eternity and, I suspect, in the new heavens and earth too. He created our taste buds, and he created amazing flavours for us to enjoy.

God also gave us the creativity to combine flavours and craft recipes that enable us to appreciate eating, which is a total sensory experience. Anyone who has spent any time in or around a kitchen knows that not only does good food involve taste, but it also involves scent, sight, sound and texture. God didn't design this "edible experience" to tempt us to gluttony, for we know that God doesn't tempt anyone (James 1:13). Like many distortions of God's earthly gifts, gluttony is both a physical and a spiritual danger; however, we need to face this "deadly sin" not through denial but rather through *right* enjoyment. Although tainted with sin, this world and the things in it are meant for our grateful and satisfied enjoyment. James tells us that "every good gift" comes from the Lord (James 1:17). When we delight in good food, we bring glory to the One who made the earth and all that is in it.

Members of the early church spent much time eating together. Today, we eat together at weddings and funerals, church functions and social engagements. Sociologists note that family meals are essential for the growth and development of healthy and happy children. Food matters, and so does the art of making food—the culinary arts. We need to value and appreciate the time invested in making good food. Parents need to teach their children how to prepare, cook and serve tasty dishes and delicacies. When we labour to create a gastronomic masterpiece, we glorify God, the one who created flavours and the one who created our senses to savour all the sights, sounds, scents, textures and tastes.

Christians are called to "taste and see that the Lord is good" (Psalm 34:8). This means not only feasting on the Word of God and delighting in him, it also means feasting on the good things created by him. So go ahead, rightly enjoy food and the art of making it wonderful. *Soli Deo gloria*!

ON ART & CREATIVITY
Love, empathy & art

This essay considers how appreciating artwork—poems, music, stories, films, paintings, etc.—can enable Christians to enter into the experiences of others. In so doing, they foster empathy and can learn to love their neighbour better, as Christ commands.[1]

Jesus tells us that the second greatest commandment is to "love your neighbour as yourself" (Mark 12:31). To love someone, you need to get to know them—know what they need, understand their strengths and weaknesses and grasp their hurts—you need to know them as well as you know your own needs, strengths, weaknesses and hurts. Knowing and loving are inextricably linked. Those who know each other well are most in love: we see love grow as people get to know each other in families, friendships and marriages.

A Christian's call to love God is also a call to know God: to know Christ more is to love him more. But what about strangers we are called to love? What about our neighbours? To "love your neighbour" means that sometimes we need to show love to people we don't "know," like the Good Samaritan who shows

---
[1] Originally published in *Barnabas*, Vol. 9, No. 3 (Summer 2017): 19.

love to the stranger in Jesus' parable (Luke 10:25–37).

How do we learn to love strangers? One of the answers, which is the focus of this essay, is to foster compassionate empathy for our fellow human beings by seeking to understand and have genuine concern for their suffering and circumstances. As with all areas of life, Jesus is the ultimate example of how we ought to live and love. On numerous occasions in the Gospels, Jesus shows "compassion" for people because of their suffering (see, for example, Matthew 9:36, Mark 8:2, Luke 7:13). Jesus' love for suffering sinners not only comes from his divine omniscience but also from his empathic experience as the Son of Man. The writer of Hebrews emphasizes the superiority of Jesus as our high priest particularly because he can "empathize with our weaknesses... [Jesus] has been tempted in every way, just as we are—yet he did not sin" (Hebrews 4:15, NIV). Biblical compassion grows out of empathy—that is, the ability to share and understand the feelings and experiences of others so that we can better help those in need.

Growing in empathy for others is one of the first lessons we learn from our kindergarten teachers: "How would you feel," asks the teacher, "if Erica didn't share the blocks with you?" The teacher is asking the little "hoarder of Lego blocks" to *empathize* with Erica; that is, to feel the way Erica is feeling. In order to be compassionate, the hoarder needs to *imagine* how Erica feels by relating to what he would feel in a similar situation. At the core of the experience is empathy. The author of Hebrews exhorts believers to "remember those who are in prison, *as though* in prison with them, and those who are mistreated, since you also are in the body" (Hebrews 13:3, emphasis mine). The author is commanding Christians to empathize with those who are suffering by imagining what it must be like to be in prison with them! So, how do we grow our *empathetic imaginations* in order to show compassion and love to our neighbour?

One way to grow our empathetic imaginations is through the arts. Art, whether paintings, poems or stories, conveys to its audience the emotional, mental and physical experiences of others. Good art should place us into the skin of another human being. One of the best forms of art for fostering empathy is literature. Dr. Peter Pikkert, professor of missions and former missionary to the Middle East, notes that when training new missionaries he advises them to read "the great literature of other nations, even in translation [because it is] one of the best ways to develop an appreciation for that people. Nothing humanizes other seemingly incomprehensible cultures more than their literature."[2] C.S. Lewis similarly writes that reading books exposes "us to experiences other than our own.... In reading great literature I become a thousand men and yet remain myself."[3] This experience, however, is also true whether you are reading a poem, seeing a play or film, contemplating a painting or sculpture, or listening to music. Different forms of art vary in intensity in conveying and teaching empathy, but all forms invite us into the feelings, thoughts and experiences of others. Jerram Barrs, apologetics professor and resident scholar of the Francis A. Schaeffer Institute, writes,

> God has not made us to be isolated individuals who find fulfillment simply by ourselves. He has made us for others so that, though finite persons, we together can reflect the unity and diversity within the godhead, and can take delight in the gifts, wisdom, and insight of our fellow men and women.[4]

We are naturally self-centred. Art, however, draws us out of ourselves and causes us to see the value of other human beings, their creativity, their experiences and their intrinsic worth as

---

[2] Peter Pikkert, email to author, August 19, 2017.
[3] C.S. Lewis, *An Experiment in Criticism* (Cambridge: Cambridge University Press, 2004), 141.
[4] Jerram Barrs, *Echoes of Eden: Reflections on Christianity, Literature, and the Arts* (Wheaton: Crossway, 2013), 29.

people made in the image of God. C.S. Lewis described the impact of art on us as "an enlargement of our being"—he argues that we want (and need) to "see with other eyes, to imagine with other imaginations, to feel with other hearts, as well as our own."[5] Sometimes we express dislike for a poem or story by stating that we can't relate to the character's experiences or the poet's feelings. But the point of the artwork isn't to magnify *our* own experiences (although that can occur) but rather to magnify someone else's experiences for us to see and better understand *them*.

Although the word "empathy" is not explicitly used in the Scriptures (unlike similar words such as compassion, sympathy and pity), the concept remains biblical: Paul commands Christians to "Rejoice with those who rejoice, weep with those who weep" (Romans 12:15). We ought to enter into the experiences of others by having our perspectives expanded through creative works of art. As we grow in our understanding of others and their experiences, we will grow in our compassion and love for our neighbours, loving as Christ commanded and loving as Christ loved us.

---

[5] C.S. Lewis, as quoted in Barrs, *Echoes of Eden*, 29.

II

ON THE ARTIST'S CALL

ON THE ARTIST'S CALL
Created to be creative

This essay considers God's call to humanity to not only enjoy the world he created, but also to add to it by being sub-creators ourselves, exercising our God-given imaginations and innovative impulses to create art, culture and even civilization itself.[1]

God first reveals himself to humanity as a creative being. Genesis is about God not only painting the universe into existence, but also weaving together the very canvas itself. From nothing God made everything. Theologians use the Latin phrase *ex nihilo*—out of nothing—to describe God's creative power. Then with a raw and formless universe, he created beauty, order and time. Out of dust and clay, God made man and placed him in a garden. Even before the foundation of the earth, God had written the story of salvation and designed the grand narrative of history. God is a creative being. Since human beings are made in the image of God, one of the attributes we inherit from our heavenly Father is his desire and ability to create. This is why we paint,

---

[1] Originally published in *Barnabas*, Vol. 9, No. 1–2 (Winter/Spring 2017): 14.

colour, draw, tell stories, make music, carve, build, design and decorate—even from our earliest age: we, too, are creative beings.

We are, however, not only made with creative abilities, we are also *commanded to create*. What is often overlooked in Genesis is one of God's earliest commissions: man is to exercise his own creativity. This is seen in two examples in the early chapters of the book. While Adam is cultivating the garden that God has made, he is also called to *name* all living creatures. Naming is an act and sign of authority; parents name children, God renames his servants and Adam names all living creatures. But naming is also an act of creativity. It was up to Adam to invent names for the creatures: we are told that God brought them to Adam "to see what he would call them" (Genesis 2:19). Whatever title Adam thought up became the creature's name. By creatively naming all creatures, Adam became a sub-creator alongside the Master Creator.

The second example of the call to creativity is in God's commission to Adam and Eve to fill the earth; this is more than calling people to have loads of babies. Timothy Keller points out that humanity's call to fill the earth means creating "civilization, not just procreation."[2] Human civilization is what we are commanded to create; God wants us to add more to the world, to continue forming it with our creativity and innovation. In so doing, we serve God through our creativity by being coworkers as well as sub-creators with him.

Take, for example, the Bible: even though it is God's Word, he commissioned and inspired numerous authors to write it using human literary genres and human authorial style and creativity. Consider the body of Christ, as manifested in the local church, which has tremendous freedom to design and organize herself within the overarching (but mostly non-prescriptive) framework outlined in the Bible. Even sermons, hymns and worship

---

[2] Timothy Keller, *Every Good Endeavor: Connecting Your Work to God's Work* (New York: Riverhead Books, 2012), 44.

services are reflective of the creative faculties of pastors, preachers, poets and other laypeople.

Creativity, then, is rooted in all areas of human existence. From the world of art, music and literature to the world of engineering, business and academics we see evidence of human creativity at work. We have been both made and commanded to create. Timothy Keller writes in his book, *Every Good Endeavor*, that one of humanity's chief purposes in Genesis is to continue cultivating the world using the materials God has made. We are called to continue the creative work God has started; as he formed the world, so we form culture, art and technology within the world. He created colour and beauty, and we create colourful and beautiful things. He created rocks and sand, and we create roads and skyscrapers. He created sound, so we create melody and music. He spoke the world into being, so we speak and write and sing "worlds" into being.

Whether you are a barista creating a cappuccino, a mathematician creating a new solution, a graphic artist creating a fresh design, an entrepreneur creating a business plan, a florist creating a bouquet, an engineer creating a bridge, a carpenter creating a cupboard, a musician creating a melody or a poet creating a poem—you are not only a creator like your heavenly Father, you are also serving him by being creative!

ON THE ARTIST'S CALL
Gifted for such a time as this

This essay explores the call of the Christian artist to use his or her gifts for Christian service within the current cultural context. Through an analogous examination of how God called and used Esther's gifts and talents in her time and place, Christian artists can be encouraged to serve God in this present time and place. There is a need for Christians within art communities not only to be a testimony through their words and actions, but also to use their artistic gifts to make known God's greatness to a new generation in need of gospel truth.[1]

Esther was an outsider who sought to live faithfully in a culture that was hostile toward her people and toward her God. During her time, the people of God were a displaced nation dispersed throughout the Persian Empire. In our own "post-Christian" culture, it often feels like we are a displaced people. Perhaps no one feels this more than the Christian who is gifted by God to be an artist. Christian artists—whether they are working on an overtly Christian project or not—will always present a Christian worldview

---

[1] Originally published in *Barnabas*, Vol. 3, No. 2 (Spring 2011): 11.

37

in their work, a worldview that is unpalatable within our present secular culture. Perhaps more disheartening for artists is the fact that the artistic medium in which they work is often misunderstood by fellow Christians. Francis Schaeffer writes, "As evangelical Christians, we have tended to relegate art to the very fringe of life."[2] *On the fringe* is not how the Bible speaks about art; in Exodus 31, being an artist is viewed as a calling!

God called Esther to use her gifts and her position to accomplish his plan and purpose. God's call on the artist is no different. Christian artists, whether they are painters, writers, musicians, graphic designers, sculptors, architects, filmmakers, etc., need to ask this question: "How does God want to use the gifts he has given to me?" Esther's example can help us answer this question.

Who we are—our gifts and talents included—is no accident. God made Esther unique in appearance and character for a purpose—*his* purpose. Like Esther, artists are "fearfully and wonderfully made" (Psalm 139:13–16) in order to use their gifts both inside and outside the church for the glory of God. But *where* and *when* we live is also no accident. Esther was made queen not only because of who she was and how she was made, but because God had engineered the circumstances and orchestrated the details of her life. Mordecai, Esther's cousin, tells her, "Who knows whether you have not attained royalty for such a time as this?" (Esther 4:14 NASB). In other words, Mordecai reminds Esther that it is no coincidence that God placed her in a unique position to help people facing a unique problem. Because God endowed her with certain gifts and talents, she has become royalty at the right time for the right reason.

Likewise, God has placed Christian artists in a media rich, visual culture for such a time as this—they are *uniquely equipped* to serve the kingdom of God here and now. With the proliferation of images, music, writing and videos on the internet and via other technologies, there is an incredible need for Christians to

---

[2] Francis A. Schaeffer, *Art and the Bible* (Downers Grove: InterVarsity Press, 2006), 13.

use media creatively to impact our present culture. This is done through the testimony of both their lives *and* the body of their work. Vocational and amateur Christian artists in Christian and non-Christian venues, ought to be "salt and light" in the theatres, art galleries, studios, newsrooms and other centres of art and culture where they produce their art. God created artists to be used by him for his kingdom…to preserve, flavour and impact the world through their art and creativity.

In the world of the arts, there are many distractions and temptations. How are Christian artists supposed to navigate within this challenging environment? Esther, in an even more dangerous environment ripe with temptations, asks Mordecai and all the Jews to "fast for me." She goes on to say, "I and my maidens also will fast in the same way" (Esther 4:16 NASB). Esther is waiting on the Lord, seeking his guidance and strength. Christian artists ought to do the same when faced with questions about how God can use their artistic talents: pray and ask others to pray. God will guide and empower each of us for such a time as this.

ON THE ARTIST'S CALL
Art for God's sake

This essay discusses the challenges faced by Christian artists when trying to reconcile their faith with their creative work. Are Christians bound to cover only explicitly Christian topics? Can God be glorified by an artist's work that doesn't convey an overtly biblical message?[1]

"*Ars gratia artis*"—"Art for art's sake."[2] This credo is held by many contemporary artists: to create art for no other purpose than simply to be art. No meaning, no message—just art as an end unto itself. To use art for some purpose, it is argued, is akin to turning it into an "advertisement" at best or "propaganda" at worst. Christian artists, however, are compelled to "do all to the glory of God" (1 Corinthians 10:31); such a view collides with the artist's mantra, "*Ars gratia artis*." How can an artist "use" his art for God without ceasing to create art? Is God only

---

[1] Originally published in *Barnabas*, Vol. 5, No. 2 (Spring 2013): 14. The title of this essay was borrowed from Philip Graham Ryken's excellent book on the subject of faith and the arts, *Art for God's Sake: A Call to Recover the Arts* (Phillipsburg: P&R Publishing, 2006).

[2] This phrase was first used in France in the early nineteenth century by philosopher Victor Cousin: "L'art pour l'art."

glorified when artists paint crosses on a hill or write choruses for the Sunday morning service?

The Israelite artists who participated in the design and creation of the Tabernacle were recognized as artists *before* they used these gifts specifically for worship (Exodus 35:10). They probably developed their artistic skills while working on "secular" projects in Egypt. This is an important point Christian artists need to realize. Artists who are Christian can sometimes feel hemmed in by their faith, believing that their art must be created for either worship or evangelism. But not every work of art created by Christian artists needs to be explicitly Christian in content. God can be glorified not only by *what* the artists convey with their art, but also by *the way* they convey it—with excellent craftsmanship, refined skill and inventiveness. When Christian artists hone the artistic skills God has given them, they glorify their Creator, the supreme Artist (Colossians 3:23; Proverbs 22:29; Ecclesiastes 9:10).

Christian artists, then, should not be limited to Christian subjects or Christian contexts; likewise, no one expects a Christian plumber to only fix church washrooms, or a Christian mechanic to only work on Christian people's cars or grocers to only sell produce mentioned in the Bible. Christian workers in any field are not hemmed in by a so-called "secular and sacred divide"—neither should Christian artists be thus restricted.

Like Christians in any vocation, however, Christian artists need to be faithful to their own worldview; this means that a Christian perspective will permeate the work of Christian artists. The way a Christian views a subject is in fact more important than the subject itself. Harry Blamires writes in *The Christian Mind*, "There is nothing in our experiences, however trivial, worldly, or even evil, which cannot be thought about christianly."[3] Christians have a much more clear perspective on the world

---

[3] Harry Blamires quoted in Leland Ryken, *The Liberated Imagination: Thinking Christianly About the Arts* (Eugene: Wipf & Stock, 2005), 248.

because they are beginning to see the cosmos as Christ sees it—that is, the world *as it truly is*. Such clarity can give poignancy and profound meaning to the works a Christian artist creates, whatever the subject matter.

Beyond creating excellent artwork, a Christian artist can also have an opportunity to be "salt and light" with his or her life. Christ has called believers to "go and make disciples" (Matthew 28:19). Oftentimes Christian artists have access to closed-off corners of the "art world" and are able to testify to God's goodness to people who rarely come in contact with true children of God. Christian artists can also glorify God by using their gifts for gainful employment—as graphic artists, fashion designers, filmmakers, architects, musicians, writers, etc. The Bible speaks a great deal about the merits of work—if you can pay the bills by making art, then do it! God is glorified when his people are diligent and industrious. The apostle Paul encourages Christians to "work with your hands" in order to support themselves (2 Thessalonians 3:12 NIV; Ephesians 4:28) and so that their "daily life may win the respect of outsiders" (1 Thessalonians 4:12 NIV).

The apostle Paul writes in Ephesians 2:10, "For we are his workmanship, created in Christ Jesus for good works, which God prepared beforehand, that we should walk in them." What good works, dear artist, has God prepared for you to do? How are you going to use your art for God's sake?

ON THE ARTIST'S CALL
Pursuing excellence in art

This essay explores the call to be creative and the need for talented artists to use and hone their gifts for the glory of God; to bring the point home, the Baroque composer and musician, J.S. Bach, is used as an exemplar of a gifted artist who didn't waste his artistic capabilities. [1]

"The invention of the arts," writes John Calvin, "is a gift of God by no means to be despised, and a faculty worthy of commendation."[2] The arts are more than hobbies; they are *gifts from God*, to be used *for* God. Take a quick glance at your church library. There you will find John Bunyan's *The Pilgrim's Progress*; maybe you will also find C.S. Lewis' *The Screwtape Letters*. Look at your hymnal, and there you will find the poetry of Isaac Watts or Fanny Crosby, and the music of Beethoven and Haydn. Flip

---

[1] Originally published in *Barnabas*, Vol. 1, No. 2 (Summer 2009): 12.
[2] John Calvin, *Commentaries on the First Book of Moses called Genesis* (Grand Rapids: Baker Books, 2003), 217. Calvin is commenting on Genesis 4:20–22: "Adah bore Jabal; he was the father of those who dwell in tents and have livestock. His brother's name was Jubal; he was the father of all those who play the lyre and pipe. Zillah also bore Tubal-cain; he was the forger of all instruments of bronze and iron. The sister of Tubal-cain was Naamah."

through your Bible; read of the craftsmen who ornamented the Tabernacle, the composers who created music or the poets who crafted the psalms. So, how do we glorify God with paintings, poems, stories or songs? One musician, whose life and work helps us answer this question, is Johann Sebastian Bach (1685–1750).

J.S. Bach used his musical gifts *extensively*. He composed over 1,000 pieces of music over his lifetime, learned to play every instrument he could lay his hands on and played them for every occasion imaginable. Bach also learned to use his gifts *extremely well*. To use your talents for the glory of God means to use them *with excellence*: so Bach was determined to hone his skills with study, practice and discipline. Today, Bach is considered to be one of the most accomplished and inventive composers in the history of music.[3]

Bach also made *all* of his music for the glory of God. He states plainly that "the aim and final end of all music should be none other than the glory of God and the refreshment of the soul."[4] All music. So, while he wrote hundreds of pieces for use in worship within the church, he also wrote beautiful concertos, humorous cantatas and musical tributes for civic festivals and private concerts. Everything he wrote declared God's greatness to the world, both inside and outside the church. Bach inscribed the letters "S.D.G." (*soli Deo gloria*—"To God alone be the glory") on many of his compositions—both sacred and secular—as a testimony to those who would perform his music; we also find inscribed the letters "J.J." (*Jesu, Juva*—"Jesus, help!") or "I.N.J." (*In nomine Jesu*—"In the name of Jesus"). Too often Christians separate their worldly callings and responsibilities from their calling to serve Christ. There is no dichotomy between the two—*everything* in the universe is under the lordship of Christ. This means we can glorify God equally well by

---

[3] See Gregory Wilbur, *Glory and Honor: The Musical and Artistic Legacy of Johann Sebastian Bach* (Nashville: Cumberland House, 2005); see also Marcus Weeks, *Music: A Crash Course* (Vancouver: Ivy Press, 1999), 50–53.

[4] J.S. Bach cited in Wilbur, *Glory and Honor*, 1.

composing beautiful music or painting a landscape as we can by writing hymns or painting a picture of Daniel in the lions' den.

Bach is a reminder to us to use with excellence the gifts God has given us. The Bible tells us to do *all things* for the glory of God. Not just "church things"...*everything*. The Bible also tells us that we are God's workmanship or handiwork (Ephesians 2:10)—this includes our intellect, bodies, interests and talents. When it comes to serving God, supporting his church or reaching out to the lost, many gifted Christians don't think of using their artistic abilities. If, however, we believe that God made us as we are, then we must also believe he intends to use us as we are: for some, that means glorifying God with a canvas or a camera, with metaphors or musical notes. Bach used the artistic gifts God gave to him to make beautiful music in honour of Christ. We should do the same with the gifts God gives to us.

ON THE ARTIST'S CALL
Don't waste your talent

This essay encourages Christians with artistic talent to use their gifts not only to create artwork that conveys biblical truth, but also to be creative in all their artistic endeavours; artists' excellence in creativity ultimately showcases God's creativity, which he freely bestowed upon humanity for our delight and his glory.[1]

You have heard it said before: "She's a talented artist" or, "He's a talented musician." What does the Bible say about talent? Jesus' parable about the *talents* (Matthew 25:14–30) is not really about "talent" the way we define the word in modern English. In fact, the word "talent" in this parable denotes a large sum of money (approximately a year's wages for a labourer). However, it doesn't take exegetical gymnastics to apply the lessons in this parable to "talents," that is, the gifts and abilities God gives to people. Jesus' overarching point is that we are given valuable gifts from God, and we are to develop, to hone and to use these gifts and resources well.

---

[1] Originally published in *Barnabas*, Vol. 6, No. 3 (Summer 2014): 14.

The psalmist David writes that God forms us, and that God knits us together in our mother's womb; in other words, we are not cosmic accidents (Psalm 139:13–16). God endows each of us with abilities and talents, which bear testimony to God's intent and purpose for each of his created beings. How we use these talents is a matter we must address. Eric Liddell ran for the glory of God, Fanny Crosby penned hymns for the glory of God and Wilberforce swayed governments for the glory of God. Each of these saints used his or her talents for God's glory.[2] If you are an artist, blessed by God with special proficiency for creating, how are you going to use these talents for the glory of God?

Like the talents in Jesus' parable, artistic ability is a precious gift that God offers to humanity. The creative impulse is valuable because is it one of the most powerful demonstrations of God's characteristic imprint on the universe. All creation testifies that he is a creative and artistic God. "The LORD God made to grow every tree that is *pleasant to the sight*" as well as "good for food" (Genesis 2:9). Artistry is a quality God values, and he means us to value it too. We are created in his image, and so we share (in varying degrees) God's creativity, his love for beauty and his desire to make things. As we exercise our creative talents by making things, we are reflecting the One in whose image we are made.

Christian artists have a special calling to use their talents well. By being excellent in their fields of expertise, Christians bring glory to God their Creator—whether it is building webpages or bird feeders, crafting sculptures or poems, or designing handbags or home interiors. Christian artists are not commanded to

---

[2] Eric Liddell (1902–1945), British Olympic champion and missionary to China; Fanny Crosby (1820–1915), American hymnwriter, who penned 9,000 hymns over her lifetime, many of which are enduring and endearing staples of modern worship (e.g., "Blessed Assurance," "To God Be the Glory," "He Hideth My Soul"); William Wilberforce (1759–1833), British antislavery politician, evangelical and philanthropist, who campaigned successfully for the abolishment of the slave trade in the British Empire (1833) and who fought for the rights and protection of child labourers, single mothers, orphans and domesticated animals among other humane causes.

use their talents only for overtly Christian purposes; however, to use their talents well means they should also find ways to use their creative abilities specifically for the advancement of the gospel and the building up of Christ's church.

John Piper urges artists, poets and musicians to "labour to say an old truth in awakening ways. God is worthy. 'Oh sing to the Lord a new song'—or picture, or poem, or figure of speech."[3] Three thousand years of recorded history bear testimony to innumerable works of art (in almost every form and genre) that have been created for the glory of God and the furtherance of his kingdom. In the twenty-first century, the church has not run out of new ways to express the great old truths about the Lord Jesus Christ and his love for the world. As the hymn stanza eloquently states,

> Could we with ink the ocean fill and were the skies of parchment made,
> Were every stalk on earth a quill and every man a scribe by trade,
> To write the love of God above would drain the ocean dry;
> Nor could the scroll contain the whole, tho' stretched from sky to sky.[4]

To tell about our wondrous Saviour is inexhaustible. Artists, don't waste your talent. Make known his greatness and his love to a new generation in new ways. Be creative for the glory of God.

---

[3] John Piper, "God Is Not Boring," *Desiring God*, February 26, 2003, www.desiringgod.org.
[4] This stanza is an English translation of a longer Jewish work by Meir Ben Isaac Nehorai (c. 1050) and was incorporated into the Christian hymn "The Love of God" (c. 1917) by Frederick M. Lehman.

ON THE ARTIST'S CALL
Helping the church get used to "all things new"

This essay presents ways that artists can help the church adjust to the "newness" of art—whether it be new approaches, new styles or different forms—without offending the very people the artist means to serve.[1]

Artists rarely work in the realm of the familiar or traditional. Instead they remix old ideas, presenting them in new and unexpected ways. Admittedly, these new and unexpected ways can sometimes appear odd. Especially within the church, new and unexpected art can sometimes evoke shock, confusion or even outrage. We are not used to new; confusing or upsetting people isn't always helpful and so artists need to remember that *loving the people of God* is more important than making art. However, serving the church with artistic creativity is important as well. If you are an artist, how can you exercise your creativity in the church without offending the ones you mean to serve? How can you labour to use your gifts for the kingdom of God while helping the church get used to "all things new"?

---

[1] Originally published as "Getting used to 'all things new'" in *Barnabas*, Vol. 6, No. 4 (Fall 2014): 14.

Firstly, prepare people for new: warn them! Provide a brief rundown of your own thinking, how you wrestled with the Scriptures, how you sought the Lord's leading while creating your art and how you want to make art for his glory and not your own. Artists sometimes forget that while working on their projects, they had ample time to "get used" to their new approaches, having already wrestled with the shock, confusion and overwhelming feelings during their own creative process. The receivers of the art, however, have not had *any* time to acclimatize to new styles or forms of art.

Secondly, you don't want your point to be lost among too much "new" and "unexpected" creativity; if the church members are befuddled and dismayed by some newfangled artistic endeavour, they will not see or hear the message your art is intended to convey. C.S. Lewis writes, "The 'unexpected' tires us: it also takes us longer to understand and enjoy than the 'expected.'"[2] In other words, less "newness" can be more powerful and engaging than incessant novelty.

Thirdly, handle traditions with appreciation, humility and respect. Tradition is important because it gives us historical perspective on the present, and it provides us with something to build on. Remember that traditions began as new innovations, and they became traditions because they worked well. Traditions often *still* work well because they are *expected*.

Fourthly, art should always "say something" to someone. Art should not be a self-indulgent and narcissistic exploration of artistic angst. Artists can be angsty and artists can be introspective. But these qualities should translate into insights for the intended audience. Here again C.S. Lewis is helpful: "All art is made to *face* the audience."[3] In other words, all forms of art—whether visual art, poetry, music, drama, literature, etc.—are made ultimately for an audience to read, listen to or view. Art is

---

[2] C.S. Lewis, *A Preface to Paradise Lost* (Oxford: Oxford University Press, 1961), 21.
[3] Lewis, *A Preface to Paradise Lost*, 20.

by nature public; it has left the private sphere of the mind and has entered the world of others.[4] Art must "face the audience," and great art can resonate powerfully with an audience. Don't waste the opportunity to make an impact on the church by not saying anything applicable or edifying to the church-at-large.

Fifthly, you should always exercise caution, being like the Bereans who searched the Scriptures to see if the words of Paul rang true (Acts 17:11). Test your art and your motives with much prayer, and saturate your work and your mind with much Scripture. You should also ask mature Christians, who have an understanding and appreciation for the arts, to provide feedback and offer mature spiritual insight.[5] Sometimes, as an artist, you may unintentionally offend by communicating something other than what you meant to convey.

Sixthly, give glory to God. He made you and endowed you with the skills and the desire to create new things. Use your gifts well for the building up of the church and the kingdom of Jesus Christ. In his name, help the church to rejoice in all things new!

---

[4] This doesn't mean that all art is publically displayed or publically available. However, even art created for private use by an artist is still "facing an audience" even if that audience happens to be the artist him- or herself. A famous example of "private art" is the writings of American poet Emily Dickenson (1830–1886). Dickenson wrote over 1,000 private poems and only published a small handful in her lifetime. Nevertheless, when Dickenson's ideas originally emerged from her imagination, flowed through her pen onto paper and were crafted into a poem, the poem became a work of art that could be read by an audience, even if that audience was only intended to be herself.

[5] It may be difficult for an artist to find mature believers who have a developed understanding of and an appreciation for the arts. Dr. Peter Pikkert suggests that artists might need to nurture a group of people he or she respects in the Lord to provide the sort of feedback the artist needs (Peter Pikkert, email to author, August 19, 2017).

III
ON LITERATURE

ON LITERATURE

Poetry, microwaves & Big Macs

This essay examines the enduring value of poetry, especially in our fast-paced, fast-food culture. The Bible urges us to "be still"—poetry can help us do just that in a world filled with distractions.[1]

"I hate poetry!" English teachers hear this phrase every time they mention the "p" word. Poetry has become synonymous with words like "confusing" and "pointless," or phrases like "out-of-date" and "hard-to-understand." If this rings true with you, then let me change the subject for a minute...to twenty-first century Western culture.

We like our communication *fast*—texts; we like our food *fast*—McDonald's; we like our cooking *fast*—microwaves. Our culture is filled with services and devices that provide ease and speedy convenience. As a result, we have come to expect everything to be fast, easy and just-a-click away. Our collective cultural "attention span" is becoming shorter by the second: when surfing the internet for example, the average viewer will spend fewer than 5 seconds on a webpage before clicking away. The problem with "fast, easy and convenient" is the accompanying

---

[1] Originally published in *Barnabas*, Vol. 2, No. 2 (Spring 2010): 10.

lack of depth, vitality and longevity. Few of us cherish emails the way we might cherish a handwritten note or letter; few of us remember the last fast-food meal or celebrate the microwave meatloaf the way we remember and celebrate Grandma's turkey dinner or homemade pie.

So what do emails, Big Macs and microwaves have to do with poetry? These icons of cultural convenience have very little to do with poetry, other than to serve as a stark contrast: poetry is anything but fast, easy or convenient. So why should Christians bother investing time and energy into understanding poetry? Because poetry helps us to slow down, ponder and understand the deep and profound realities of God's universe. While our culture is chock-full of vapid, ephemeral experiences, God's creation is full of inspiring, rich and eternal experiences. "Be still," the psalmist writes, "and know that I am God" (Psalm 46:10). In our fast-paced, non-stop, 24/7 culture, reading poetry teaches us to slow down and "be still." Poetry instills in us the habit of remembering and reflecting on who we are, who God is, and what life is all about.

Poetry is also a powerful way to express the wonder, depth and beauty of God's world and to capture the essence of our human experience. Nowhere is this more evident than in the poetry of the Bible. The great poems of the Psalms have been the mainstay of many Christians through times of trial and joy; the depth and profundity of the Psalms are in part due to the medium of poetry. This is true with hymns as well; Christians cherish the poetry of hymns sung weekly during church meetings. But our enjoyment of poetry should not be limited to the psalms or to hymns. All great poets are great observers; they hold up a mirror to ourselves and to society, so they have much to teach us about life on earth. In a powerful way, they urge us to stop and reflect on our human experience, God's universe and his goodness to us in a world mired in sin.

As we read a broad range of poetry, both secular and sacred, we will be challenged to look at ourselves and God's world with fresh perspectives. Our ability to appreciate the Psalms and hymnody will also be enhanced by concerted attention to all kinds of poems. Most importantly, perhaps, we will learn to pause in our hectic lives in order to take in the beauty and wonder of God's creation.

Here are some poets worth investing time in: John Donne, George Herbert, Christina Rossetti, T.S. Eliot, John Milton, William Shakespeare, Edmund Spenser, Anne Bradstreet and Robert Herrick.

ON LITERATURE
Why we should read fiction

This essay argues for our need to read and understand stories. Many Christians prefer reading nonfiction books on overt Christian themes and topics, such as theology, biography or Christian living. However, fiction can fire our imaginations and provide new insights into our own experiences and the experiences of others.[1]

"Be very careful, then," Paul writes to the Ephesians, "how you live—not as unwise but as wise, making the most of every opportunity, because the days are evil" (Ephesians 5:15–16 NIV). A Christian who takes seriously Paul's warning might wonder whether reading works of fiction (eg., novels, plays and poetry) is a good use of his or her time. Even C.S. Lewis—who devoted much of his career and life to the study of fiction—writes, "The Christian knows from the outset that the salvation of a single soul is more important than the production or preservation of all the epics and tragedies in the world."[2] The argument follows, then, that Christians should instead devote themselves to the Scriptures

---

[1] Originally published in *Barnabas*, Vol. 7, No. 4 (Fall 2015): 22.
[2] C.S. Lewis, *Christian Reflections*, ed. Walter Hooper (London: Fount, 1998), 12.

and to reading important works of theology, Christian spirituality and the biographies of saints. In other words, we should invest our time reading books about real events and real concerns.

The problem is that God made us to delight in *stories*. We learn best from stories. Sometimes the most winning and clearest portions of a theology book are anecdotes—small stories—illustrating the point being made. Stories are powerful teachers because they *show* rather than *tell*. The parables of Jesus are great examples of the power of literary imagination to teach complex and mysterious truths. Consider also the compelling tale told by Nathan the prophet to awaken King David to the depth of his sin with Bathsheba (2 Samuel 12).[3]

The Scriptures as a whole use story elements and contain both historical and fictional stories. Eugene Peterson observes,

> Story is the primary way in which the revelation of God is given to us. The Holy Spirit's literary genre of choice is story. Story isn't a simple or naïve form of speech from which we graduate to the more sophisticated 'higher' languages of philosophy or mathematics. The biblical story comprises other literary forms—sermons and genealogies, prayers and letters, poems and proverbs—but story carries them all.[4]

The Bible is a literary work—divinely inspired, unique and true—but still it is a book that tells the "old, old story" using literary elements.

Stories also grow out of our human creativity, and God himself is the supreme creative one. Our creative impulse is derived from him. He is the great storyteller; we who are created in his image simply reflect this attribute of our maker. Francis Schaeffer writes,

---

[3] See page 85 for more about Nathan's interactions with King David.
[4] Eugene H. Peterson, *Leap Over a Wall: Earthly Spirituality for Everyday Christians* (San Francisco: HarperCollins, 1997), 3.

If Christianity is really true, then it involves the whole man, including his intellect and creativeness. Christianity is not just 'dogmatically' true or 'doctrinally' true. Rather, it is true to what is there, true in the whole area of the whole man in all of life.[5]

If we limit ourselves to only one sort of reading, then we miss out on a richer and fuller understanding of the Christian experience in this world, an experience that includes creativity.

God has not called us to retreat to intellectual monasteries where we only read doctrine and theology; rather, we are to engage and understand the world that God has placed us in. One of the best ways to understand our world and our fellow human beings is to read the best works of literature available. You will learn more about humanity, you will learn a great deal about yourself, and you will enrich your appreciation of our creative God who made us with creative hearts and minds!

---

[5] Francis A. Schaeffer, *Art and the Bible* (Downers Grove: InterVarsity Press, 2006), 16.

ON LITERATURE

Narnia, Harry Potter & *Lord of the Rings*: Are there "bad" stories?

This essay considers how Christians can navigate the increasingly popular world of fantasy and science fiction stories and films by considering the question, "Is there such a thing as a bad story?" [1]

The *Chronicles of Narnia, The Hunger Games, Harry Potter, The Game of Thrones, The Lord of the Rings*.... It seems fantasy and science fiction books (and films) are taking our culture by storm, and if you have children, ignoring these sorts of books and films isn't an option. Large sections of local bookstores are dominated by books and paraphernalia springing from these genres. Overnight, these authors become millionaires; their stories inspire blockbuster movie franchises and countless toys, confectionaries, souvenirs and, every once and while, a theme park too. With all this fanfare about science fiction and fantasy books, there has been an equal amount of controversy. As Christians who have been called to be *in* the world, we cannot ignore these cultural powerhouses; but as Christians set apart by God,

---

[1] Originally published as "Stories: What is the message?" in *Barnabas*, Vol.4, No. 2 (Spring 2012): 14.

we are not to be *of* the world. For the sake of ourselves, our families and those we are trying to reach with the gospel, we need to be concerned with and aware of the powerful influence stories (and storytellers) can have in shaping our values, our thinking and our worldview.

Christians are notoriously inconsistent in trying to manage the influence of stories. *Harry Potter*, for example, has been denounced because there are wizards and witches; but there are also wizards and witches in the *Narnia* chronicles and in *The Lord of the Rings*. These stories are much beloved in many Christian circles. Some denounce *Harry Potter* because of the "pagan mythological elements" yet embrace the explicitly pagan classics of literature. Some condemn *Harry Potter* but embrace the seemingly benign, but often more harmful, individualistic sentimentalism of Disney films. Some reject the "fantasy" genre altogether, although many Christian authors have used the fantasy genre as a powerful medium to express Christian truth: these include celebrated authors such as John Bunyan, Edmund Spenser, George MacDonald, C.S. Lewis, Madeleine L'Engle and J.R.R. Tolkien.

God is the standard for morality. But how do we measure the morality of a book against God's standard? Counting witches or pagan elements or wrong behaviour isn't the answer. The Bible contains murder, violence, genocide, rape, deception, stealing and pagan religions...just to name a few. The morality of a book is not necessarily connected with what it *contains*, but what it *conveys*.

When evaluating a story, the most important question to ask is whether the messages and the worldview presented by the story *are true*. If a novel presents a "truth" that is contrary to God's created reality, then a Christian can safely argue that the book is immoral. Some fantasy novelists attempt to recast reality by "redefining" what "good" is rather than acknowledging that good is defined by the immutable God. An example of an author's attempt to reshape reality is in the popular children's fantasy novel *The Golden Compass* by Philip Pullman. His novel contains many fantasy elements similar to those found in C.S. Lewis' *Narnia* books—talking animals, parallel worlds, a human child navigating a magical realm, even a wardrobe; the difference, however, is the message. In Pullman's novel, Christianity is overtly portrayed as negative and even harmful; in its place, Pullman champions a hedonistic, man-centred, new-age spiritualism, which he presents as positive and real. Teaching this anti-Christian sentiment to children is at the heart of his storytelling. "All stories teach," Pullman rightly states. "They teach the morality we live by." So what is he teaching? In the most unequivocal manner possible, Pullman asserts, "My books are about killing God."[2]

Stories are a gift from God. Like all gifts from God, they can be used for good—teaching us, encouraging us, delighting us—or they can be used for evil. Whether there are wizards or wardrobes, ask yourself—*What is the message?*

---

[2] Steve Meacham, "The Shed Where God Died," *The Sydney Morning Herald*, December 13, 2003, http://www.smh.com.au/articles/2003/12/12/1071125644900.html

ON LITERATURE
Monsters in the mirror

This essay examines the lessons Christians can learn from "made-up" monsters in literature and fairy tales. Monsters point to the deeper and real danger of unchecked evil—that is, sin in our lives and in the world we live in.[1]

In nearly every epic story, fairy tale or adventure film there are monsters of one kind or another. Bilbo Baggins in *The Hobbit* has Gollum, trolls and a dragon. Luke Skywalker in *Star Wars* has Darth Vader. The boy wizard Harry Potter has Voldemort. The Anglo-Saxon hero Beowulf has Grendel. Little Red Riding Hood has the Big Bad Wolf. Why do we fill our stories with larger-than-life monsters? Do made-up monsters have anything to teach Christians?

In his critical essay *Beowulf: The Monsters and the Critics*, J.R.R. Tolkien argues that the monsters in literature are more than entertaining enemies for heroes to demonstrate their strength; monsters are essential to life and literature as they can teach us about our own humanity.[2] Tolkien's assessment of our

---

[1] Originally published in *Barnabas*, Vol. 8, No. 4 (Fall 2016): 20.
[2] J.R.R. Tolkien, *The Monsters and the Critics and Other Essays* (London: HarperCollins, 2006), 5–48.

need for monsters is further underscored by the fact that our English word *monster* ultimately derives from the Latin word, *monstrum*, which means "a warning," "a sign," "an omen." Michael Poteet further points out that this Latin word also gives us the English verb "to monitor," which means "to observe" and "check" the progress or quality of something or someone.[3]

Literary monsters can serve as warnings and monitors of our behaviour by enabling us to see the ugliness of evil more clearly and reflecting back important insights into the state of our own hearts. Monsters are like mirrors of our sinful selves; they depict on the "outside" what is going on in the "inside." In other words, trolls, orcs and dragons look as evil and nasty as they really are on the "inside": their revolting appearance and actions remind us how offensive sin really is. C.S. Lewis demonstrates this well in his novel *The Voyage of the Dawn Treader*, when a greedy and self-absorbed child turns into a dragon: "Sleeping on a dragon's hoard with greedy, dragonish thoughts in his heart, he had become a dragon himself" writes Lewis' narrator.[4] The boy's outside appearance now looks like the state of his inward self. Herein lies the biblical lesson: monsters serve as warnings of not only what we *all* could become but also of what we are… apart from the grace of God. Monsters remind us that we need Christ to intervene and transform our lives into something good and beautiful.

Essentially monsters serve as a metaphor for evil and sin; they dwell in a "black and white" literary landscape where the only common ground between good and evil is the battleground. In our present culture, people struggle with monsters as metaphors for evil and sin because most individuals don't believe "evil" and "sin" exist. People believe that the world consists mainly of "grey" areas; differentiating good and evil is for fairy tales and fanciful religions. But the Bible is clear about good and evil; both are real and there is no compromise between the two.

---

3 Michael Poteet, *Beowulf Study Guide* (Fall Creek: Progeny Press, 2011), 56.
4 C.S. Lewis, *The Voyage of the Dawn Treader* (New York: HarperCollins, 2000), 91.

Herein lies the second lesson about sin and evil we can learn from monsters: like monsters, sin must be destroyed. There is no appeasing or tolerating the Orcs of Mordor or the Dragon under The Lonely Mountain. There is no "peace accord" that can be made between Beowulf and Grendel. *The monster must always be destroyed.* Similarly, the apostle Paul exhorts us, "Put to death therefore what is earthly in you" (Colossians 3:5). "For if you live according to the flesh you will die, but if by the Spirit you put to death the deeds of the body, you will live" (Romans 8:13). We are called to take up the cross, and the cross is a means of putting our ambitions and sinful desires to death. In other words, the monster we see in the mirror is a monster that must be slain.

Reading epic masterpieces about heroes and monsters won't save us, but it can point us to our sinful selves, our need for healing and redemption, and our ongoing spiritual battle for holiness and righteousness. Next time you see the monster in the mirror, don't be "like someone who looks at his face in a mirror and, after looking at himself, goes away and immediately forgets what he looks like" (James 1:23–24 NIV). In Christ's name and by the power of his Spirit, slay the monster that resides in your heart. Or, as John Owen writes, "Be killing sin or it will be killing you."[5]

---

[5] John Owen, *The Works of John Owen* (16 vols., 1967 reprint; Edinburgh: Banner of Truth, 1853) 6:177, 6:9.

ON LITERATURE
Bunyan's *The Pilgrim's Progress*

This essay considers the enduring legacy of the great seventeenth-century allegory by John Bunyan and why we still need to read (and re-read) it today.[1]

One of the most published and widely recognized books of all time is John Bunyan's *The Pilgrim's Progress*. Since its first appearance in 1678, the impact of Bunyan's masterpiece on the church of Jesus Christ is incalculable. The famous nineteenth-century poet preacher C.H. Spurgeon read *The Pilgrim's Progress* over 100 times during his lifetime, and he regularly encouraged saints to read and re-read it.[2] C.S. Lewis, the author of the *Chronicles of Narnia*, called *The Pilgrim's Progress* "a book that has astonished the whole world."[3] Even the famous twentieth-century agnostic playwright, George Bernard Shaw, stated that

---

[1] Originally published in *Barnabas*, Vol. 6, No. 2 (Spring 2014): 22.
[2] Thomas Spurgeon, introduction to C.H. Spurgeon, *Pictures from The Pilgrim's Progress: A Commentary on Portions of John Bunyan's Immortal Allegory* (Pasadena: Pilgrim Publications, 1992), 5.
[3] C.S. Lewis, *Mere Christianity: Comprising the Case for Christianity, Christian Behaviour, and Beyond Personality* (New York: HarperCollins, 1998), 75.

Bunyan's novel greatly influenced him (he had portions of it read at his funeral), and Shaw believed it surpassed the works of William Shakespeare in quality, form and style.[4]

John Bunyan's *The Pilgrim's Progress* is an allegory, meaning that the characters, settings and events in the book hold symbolic significance beyond the story itself. The story represents a Christian's journey of faith by following the adventures of a redeemed pilgrim, who was once named "Graceless" but who now bears the name "Christian." Like all who call on the name of the Lord, Christian is fleeing his hometown ("The City of Destruction"), and he is heading toward the wonderful City of God. Along the "narrow" way, he encounters many temptations, many foes of his faith, and many faithful friends, each symbolizing the real challenges all Christians face and the real help God gives his people as they seek to live according to the Way.

Although it is a work of marvellous fiction, *The Pilgrim's Progress* is biblically saturated: there are over 200 direct quotations from the Bible, as well as countless paraphrases, references and allusions. About Bunyan's biblical richness, Spurgeon states,

> Why, this man [Bunyan] is a living Bible! Prick him anywhere, and you will find that his blood is Bibline, the very essence of the Bible flows through him. He cannot speak without quoting a text, for his soul is full of the Word of God.[5]

One of the great strengths of Bunyan's book is its ability to convey complicated theological truths in a clear and simple way. C.S. Lewis praises Bunyan's unencumbered style of writing: "the light is sharp; it never comes through stained glass."[6] In other

---

[4] E.E. Stokes, "Bernard Shaw's Debt to John Bunyan," *The Shaw Review* 8, No. 2 (1965): 42–51, www.jstor.org/stable/40682054.
[5] Thomas Spurgeon, introduction Spurgeon, *Pictures from The Pilgrim's Progress*, 6.
[6] C.S. Lewis, *Selected Literary Essays*, ed. Walter Hooper (Cambridge: Cambridge University Press, 1980), 148.

words, Bunyan preaches without being "preachy"; he exposes human sin and foolishness without a "holier-than-thou" disposition. Nevertheless, there is no "tickling of ears" here: sin is squarely addressed as loathsome to God, and Bunyan's characters—who bear names reflecting their wickedness and folly—are clearly condemned. The difference is that Bunyan gives us warnings in a sincere, compassionate and humble manner. He writes with the heart of a pastor who lovingly cares for his flock.

Beyond its richness in theological truths and spiritual applications, *The Pilgrim's Progress* is a superb story—that is, entertaining, engaging and exciting. Leland Ryken, professor emeritus of literature at Wheaton College, notes, "The book is like Homer's *Odyssey* or Tolkien's *Lord of the Rings*—a continuous series of narrow escapes and threatening ordeals."[7]

Similar to life itself, John Bunyan's *The Pilgrim's Progress* contains moments of electrifying adventure, deep despair, great delight, gripping sadness and enjoyable humour. Woven into the fabric of his story, Bunyan beautifully entwines the spiritual, psychological and physical aspects of the human and Christian experience. With biblical insight into the heart of humanity, Bunyan portrays an admonishing, encouraging and instructive narrative of what it means to be a real Christian in this world. Pick it up, read it, enjoy it and learn from it!

Readers who are less familiar with the King James Version of the Bible may have difficulty with the original seventeenth-century English edition of The Pilgrim's Progress. *There are, however, many updated and revised versions of* The Pilgrim's Progress *available today. Recommended edition:* The Pilgrim's Progress in Modern English *revised by L. Edward Hazelbaker—"sensitively revised for the 21st century reader"—which includes explanatory notes, a timeline and a study guide.*

---

[7] Leland Ryken, *Bunyan's The Pilgrim's Progress*, Christian Guides to the Classics (Wheaton: Crossway, 2014), 13.

ON LITERATURE
Shakespeare's world(view)

This essay explores the Christian worldview that underpins Shakespeare's plays. This biblical lens through which Shakespeare observed the world and his fellow humanity is what makes his works universally relevant across time and space, bridging cultural and geographic divides for the last four centuries.[1]

...God shall be my hope,
My stay, my guide and lantern to my feet.
—*Henry VI* (II.iii)

Was William Shakespeare a Christian? The truth is we really don't know much about him at all. What we do know is that his poetry and plays are among the most celebrated works of literature in the world. Despite the facts that his historical and literary allusions are often obscure, his language is challenging and his plays are over 400 years old, Shakespeare remains a vital part of our culture.

---

[1] Originally published in *Barnabas*, Vol. 2, No. 3 (Summer 2010): 10.

Should Christians pay attention to Shakespeare? One reason to do so is that Shakespeare's plays are beautiful poetry—and since creativity and beauty are attributes of God, Christians should be interested in all things of beauty. A second reason is that Shakespeare is part of the culture we are trying to reach with the gospel—his plays are taught in nearly every school in the English-speaking world, and his works are still performed in nearly every region around the globe. Like the apostle Paul preaching on Mars Hill in Athens, we can refer to one of "your own poets" when presenting the gospel (Acts 17:28).

The value of Shakespeare for Christians, however, goes even deeper than its beauty or cultural relevance. Shakespeare's works are rich in biblical truth: biblical themes abound in Shakespeare's plays, from salvation to providence to grace. Many Christians are surprised to discover that "grace working in a fallen world" is a main theme in Shakespeare's plays.

> O, if men were to be saved by merit, what hole in hell were hot enough for him?
> —*Henry IV*, Part 1 (II.i)

> A double blessing is a double grace.
> —*Hamlet* (I.iii)

Upon the stage, man's rebellious nature is pitted against God's sovereignty. What unfolds is the working out of grace, providence and sometimes tragedy. Ironically, postmodern relativists would fit nicely into one of Shakespeare's plays...not as a hero, however, but as a villain! From Lady Macbeth to *Hamlet*'s Claudius, many of Shakespeare's villains try to redefine the universe to suit their purposes and reduce God to their own image. But there is no more room for relativism in Shakespeare's world than there is in God's world.

In the great hand of God I stand.
—*Macbeth* (II.iii)

But he, that hath the steerage of my course,
Direct my sail!
—*Romeo and Juliet* (I.iv)

William Shakespeare was a gifted writer, not only in his ability to beautifully craft the English language, but also because of his ability to accurately observe, understand and describe reality. He was a keen observer of God's creation, and he reflected God's world when creating his own for the stage.

Much of the world's literature tells us a great deal about the authors themselves: what they thought, what they believed, what they valued. Shakespeare's works are unique in that they tell us very little about the author and a great deal about the real world we live in. Shakespeare's world is a fallen world, a world where "we are sinners all."[2] Granted, Elizabethan England—the time and place Shakespeare wrote his plays—was a Christianized culture; the Christian elements in his plays, however, are more than the mere window dressings of Shakespeare's cultural context. The events in his plays unfold in a world baptized by the Christian imagination and shaped by mercy and grace, and in a universe ruled by a sovereign God. So dust off your annotated Shakespeare or catch a play at the local theatre, and be blessed by England's greatest bard.

Recommended resource: Peter Leithart's Brightest Heaven of Invention: A Christian Guide to Six Shakespearean Plays.

---

[2] *Henry IV*, Part 2 (III.iii).

ON LITERATURE
Imagining reality in *Hamlet*

This essay compares the power of storytelling in Shakespeare's Hamlet *to the power of parable told by the prophet Nathan in 2 Samuel. Our imaginations are designed by God to be awakened by storytelling to help us come to a deeper understanding of both righteousness and sin.*[1]

The central reason for Shakespeare's continued appeal over the last four centuries is his ability to depict reality, to give a true portrait of the real universe— God's universe. This is especially true in Shakespeare's deep and profound presentation of who we are as human beings—creatures created in the image of God. Essentially, Shakespeare's plays give us insight into the human condition. It is important to note that Shakespeare's portrayal of reality is not hackneyed like so-called contemporary "reality" TV programs, which seem to revel in all things bizarre and meaningless. Rather, Shakespeare's portrayal of reality is rich, textured and sharply perceptive. If Shakespeare truly speaks about the universal truths of the human experience, then his

---

[1] Originally published in *Barnabas*, Vol. 6, No. 1 (Winter 2014): 22.

plays should resonate with people wherever and whenever they are found. This was the case for convicted criminals who were serving time at the Missouri Eastern Correctional Center. These prisoners participated in a performing arts program in which they studied, explored and performed in a "jailhouse" production of Shakespeare's *Hamlet*. Some may ask what connections the 400-year-old drama by Shakespeare could have with twenty-first century hardened criminals serving time in prison. However, Jill Carattini of Ravi Zacharias International Ministries notes the impact this Shakespearean play had on the inmates as they studied and performed it:

> ...Over the course of six months, a prison performing arts program gave a handful of criminals, who are living out the consequences of their violent crimes, the chance to delve into a story about a man pondering a violent crime and its consequences. The result was a startling encounter for both the players, most of whom were new to Shakespeare.... One man, in order to play the character Laertes, found himself reckoning with the temptation to manipulate as a means of getting what you want, only to realize a kind of cowardice in such actions. In a moment of clarity through the life of another, he admits, "I can identify with that [struggle] and I can play that role very well—because I've been playing that role my whole life.... To put a gun in somebody's face—that's an unfair advantage. That's a cowardly act. And that's what criminals are; we're cowards." He then admits with striking transparency, "I am Laertes. I am. I am."[2]

What is most powerful about this story is how a fictional character impressed upon the convict's heart the true nature of his actions and his crimes.[3] All the legal statements and court

---

[2] Jill Carattini, "Who Is Laertes?" Ravi Zacharias International Ministries, May 9, 2011, http://rzim.org/a-slice-of-infinity/who-is-laertes/.
[3] In Shakespeare's play *Hamlet*, the character Laertes engages in what seems like an

proceedings, media articles, victim impact statements—even a cold, hard prison cell—failed to show him the deep, cowardly reality of his crime. It took a story, a 400-year-old story, to awaken his soul and his mind to reality.

This is similar to the story told by the prophet Nathan after King David commits adultery with a woman named Bathsheba; she was already married to a man named Uriah, who was a faithful captain in David's army. When Bathsheba becomes pregnant with David's child, David makes several attempts to cover up his crime. In the end, he orders the death of Uriah in order to take Bathsheba as his wife (2 Samuel 11). God uses the prophet Nathan to awaken King David to the full weight of the sin the king has committed. Instead of coming to David directly with the proclamation of guilt, Nathan tells a story. He tells a parable of a rich man's selfish and unjust treatment of a poor man, which King David took to be a true, literal account; the king's reaction was that of outrage and cries for justice. Then Nathan said, "You are the man!" (2 Samuel 12:7). David had failed to see the wickedness of his adultery and scheme of murder up until this moment, when he is confronted with his sin in the context of a story.

Stories are a powerful way to awaken us to the timeless truths that exist within the universe created by God. Even in Shakespeare's play, *Hamlet*, the pensive Prince Hamlet uses drama to elicit the guilt of the murderous King Claudius: Hamlet calls for a play to be performed before the king that resembles the murder of Claudius' predecessor. Hamlet states,

...the play's the thing
Wherein I'll catch the conscience of the king.
—*Hamlet* (Act II, Scene ii)

---

honest fencing match between himself and the character Hamlet. However, Laertes secretly uses a real sword with a poisoned tip in order to murder Hamlet. Betrayal, deception and cowardice are major themes in the play.

Like King David when confronted with Nathan's story, Shakespeare's Claudius is also confronted with the reality of his crimes through imaginative storytelling.

This is why God created humanity with an imagination—not to waste on wishful thinking or empty dreaming—but to gain a deeper understanding and clearer picture of reality. Jill Carattini writes,

> Jesus places us beside images of a kingdom that turns things around, stories that shock and offend us, metaphors that wake us to the presence of a surprising God, to the mindsets and pieties that block us from seeing this God, and to the abundance of divine grace that beckons us to look again and again.[4]

May you exercise your imagination when you read Shakespeare and when you read the Scriptures, and may the Lord use story to awaken your mind and soul to new and forgotten truths.

---

4 Carattini, "Who Is Laertes?"

ON LITERATURE

Jane Austen: Small joys & simple pleasures

This essay considers the Christian legacy that Jane Austen presents in her novels. Through the subtle portrayal of characters, events and themes and by focusing on the simple pleasures and small joys of life, Austen shows us how to recognize these blessings God provides in our day-to-day lives.[1]

Jane Austen (1775–1817), the author of *Pride and Prejudice*, remains one of the world's most celebrated writers. She is praised by academics, who studiously examine her works in universities and high schools and write reams of essays and articles on the finer points of her masterpieces. She is also adored by countless readers—both male and female—who read and re-read her novels time and again. New readers are constantly added to Jane Austen's fanbase, as thousands of her novels are sold each year around the globe. Her six novels have not been out of print since they first appeared over 200 years ago. All of her novels have been made into multiple television mini-series' and successful Hollywood films. But Austen's enduring importance goes well beyond academic inquiry,

---

[1] Originally published in *Barnabas*, Vol. 5, No. 1 (Winter 2013): 14.

popularity or mere escapist entertainment. Austen's novels address fundamentally human concerns and can provide great insight into what it means to be a Christian in a fallen world, especially a world painted with a veneer of order and civility.

Jane Austen lived during one of the most tumultuous times in history—the American Revolution, the French Revolution, the Industrial Revolution—events that take centre stage in history books. All of her novels are also set during the period of the Napoleonic Wars, when England was under constant threat of defeat by France or even invasion by Napoleon's forces. However, in her books she rarely makes mention of this or any other major historical event. In fact, "nothing" really happens in Austen's novels at all! No explosions, no duels to the death and no "high adrenaline" horse-and-carriage chases.[2] One critic notes that no one even bleeds in an Austen novel.[3] Yet her novels are in no way "boring," nor is Austen an out-of-touch idealist presenting life as trouble-free and idyllic like a painting by American sentimental artist Thomas Kinkade.

But Austen was no naïve nostalgist, lost in the romantic past, nor was she a sentimentalist. She simply urges her readers to delight in the small but immensely enjoyable moments that make up the present. In reality, our lives consist mostly of small moments and little events. Even during the difficult and challenging times, God provides soothing balms—sometimes in small doses—if we have eyes to see them. Austen teaches us to find joy in these subtle gifts from God. As Christians, we are called to live sincere and simple lives (1 Thessalonians 4:11). This is the life Austen portrays beautifully in her novels. C.S. Lewis writes that Austen

> envisages no grandiose schemes of joy. She has, or at least all her favourite characters have, a hearty relish for what

---

[2] Peter J. Leithart, *Miniatures and Morals: The Christian Novels of Jane Austen* (Moscow: Canon Press, 2004), 20.
[3] Leithart, *Miniatures and Morals*, 18.

would now be regarded as very modest pleasures. A ball, a dinner party, books, conversation, a drive to see a great house ten miles away, a holiday as far as Derbyshire—these, with affection (that is essential) and good manners, are happiness. She is no Utopian.[4]

This is a useful lesson for Christians, and it can be an antidote for much discouragement. When we look for tidal waves of blessings we miss the "morning dew moments" God provides.

But Austen not only helps us to delight in small joys and simple pleasures, she also reveals the ugliness of "small" sins, what Jerry Bridges calls "respectable sins."[5] In Austen's novels, men and women can be villainous without wearing black hats, kidnapping damsels or offering up poison-laced apples. In fact, villainy can seem quite respectable at times. Austen forces her readers to see the repulsiveness of less obvious sins; offences such as sin of omission, sins of the tongue and sins of attitude. What we *don't do* for others, how we speak *about* others or the way we speak *to* others, how we care for those in need, how we react to the minor annoyances of life…even our persistent "pride" and our subtle "prejudices"—these behaviours and attitudes can make us villains in the eyes of God and men. We need to reflect God's goodness and grace in both word and deed (Colossians 3:17), both in attitude and action (1 John 3:18). These biblical themes are powerfully illustrated in Austen's novels. So recline with a cup of tea and a Jane Austen novel. Learn how to be faithful in small ways, to delight in small pleasures, always remembering that sin is sin, no matter how respectable it may seem.

Recommended resource: Peter Leithart's Miniatures and Morals: The Christian Novels of Jane Austen.

---

[4] C.S. Lewis, "A Note on Jane Austen," in *A Truth Universally Acknowledged: 33 Great Writers on Why We Read Jane Austen*, ed. Susannah Carson (New York: Random House, 2010), 114.

[5] Jerry Bridges, *Respectable Sins: Confronting the Sins We Tolerate* (Colorado Springs: NavPress, 2007).

IV

ON MUSIC

ON MUSIC
Reforming music: Bach & Luther

This essay considers the influence of Martin Luther and the Reformation on the creative works of the great Baroque composer, J.S. Bach.[1]

Johann Sebastian Bach (1685–1750) is considered to be one of the greatest composers of Western music; he is also considered to be one of the world's most creative geniuses. Many music historians agree that without Bach, we wouldn't have Beethoven, Brahms or Mozart. It has also been stated, however, that without Martin Luther, the great German Reformer of the sixteenth century, there would have been no Bach. The musical "formations" of Bach's day grew out of the theological "reformations" of Luther's day. Musicologist Carroll Moulton writes, "[Bach] represents the culmination of a stream of Protestant church music that had developed since the start of the Reformation in the early sixteenth century."[2] It is not hard to see the connections between these two great men of God.

---

[1] Originally published in *Barnabas*, Vol. 7, No. 1 (Winter 2015): 14.
[2] Carroll Moulton, *Music in Time: A Survey of Western Music* (Princeton: Films for the Humanities, 1983).

J.S. Bach lived in Germany during what is known as the Baroque period, a time of remarkable creativity in all of the arts. Bach's family was also very musical; his family lineage boasts seven generations of professional musicians. In some parts of Germany, the name "Bach" was synonymous with the word "musician."[3] But biographer Gregory Wilbur notes that Bach's family members were also faithful followers of Jesus Christ and they adhered to the reformed faith.[4] Fleeing religious persecution, Bach's family migrated to the region of Thuringia, a stronghold of reformed faith and a bastion of brilliant ecclesiastical music. This "stronghold" is where Bach grew up and attended school. It is also the region where Martin Luther spent his youth. Both Bach and Luther attended the same Latin School in Eisenach—albeit 200 years apart![5] Bach also spent his days in the shadows of Wartburg Castle, perched high above Eisenach, where in the previous century, Luther hid from his enemies and where he translated the Greek New Testament into German. These tangible reminders of Luther's Reformation must have left an indelible impression on the young Bach. But more powerful, perhaps, was the influence of Luther's views upon J.S. Bach's own appreciation of music.

Martin Luther writes, "Next to the Word of God, music deserves the highest praise. I plainly judge, and do not hesitate to affirm, that except for theology, there is no art that could be put on the same level with music."[6] For Luther, music was an incredibly inspiring and powerful gift from God. However, it was not simply "music for music's sake." Luther believed that music aided and enhanced the Christian's worship of the great and mighty Creator. Luther states,

---

[3] Paul Johnson, *Creators: From Chaucer and Dürer to Picasso and Disney* (New York: HarperCollins, 2006), 77.
[4] See Gregory Wilbur, *Glory and Honor: The Musical and Artistic Legacy of Johann Sebastian Bach* (Nashville: Cumberland House, 2005).
[5] Wilbur, *Glory and Honor*, 6.
[6] Martin Luther quoted in Wilbur, *Glory and Honor*, 5.

God has cheered our hearts and minds through his dear Son, whom he gave us to redeem us from sin, death and the devil. He who believes this cannot be quiet about it. But he must gladly and willingly sing and speak about it so others also may come to hear it. And whoever does not want to sing and speak of it shows that he does not believe.[7]

Luther sought to apply his ideas about music and worship to actual church music; as a result, he was a prolific hymnwriter. Luther's hymns proved to be a great spiritual and musical inspiration for Bach throughout his life. He perused Luther's hymns for comfort, theological instruction and for lyrics to articulate his own devotion to God. Bach adapted many of Luther's hymns when composing his copious cantatas—he wrote over 200! Bach was most influenced by Luther's determination to incorporate music into the life of the church. This is why Bach's church music was designed to be "accessible" to his congregation by using familiar hymns in his cantatas. Reverence was also a key aspect of Bach's church music compositions. In the margins of Bach's personal Bible, beside 2 Chronicles 5:13, he inscribed, "At a reverent performance of music, God is always at hand with his gracious presence."[8] This is the heart of Bach's pursuit of excellence in music.

J.S. Bach's biographer, Paul Johnson, observes that although "Bach was a Lutheran by birth, education, taste, and, not least, loyalty," he was, "in a deeper sense...a Christian."[9] Bach has even been called the "fifth evangelist" and a "theologian who worked with a keyboard."[10] Musically and lyrically, Bach created works that radiate theological truths. This is no coincidence; Bach intentionally composed with theological truths at the forefront

---

[7] Martin Luther quoted in Wilbur, *Glory and Honor*, 5–6.
[8] "Johann Sebastian Bach: The Fifth Evangelist" in Mark Galli and Ted Olsen, eds., *131 Christians Everyone Should Know* (Nashville: Holman, 2000), 109.
[9] Johnson, *Creators*, 84.
[10] Galli and Olsen, eds., *131 Christians Everyone Should Know*, 109.

of his mind. Bach's personal library contained eighty volumes of theological works over and above his extensive musical library. He was known to be well versed in sound theology. Robin Leaver notes that Bach sincerely held to the central doctrines of the Reformation: "*sola scriptura, sola gratia* and *sola fide*: that is, one's standing before God rests not with the authority of the church but on the authority of scripture; that one's salvation…depends upon the grace of God in Christ, rather than human endeavour; and that salvation can only be appropriated by faith"—Bach signed a statement indicating that he subscribed to these beliefs and none other.[11] Without a doubt, there was no distinction between theology and the music Bach created.

Most notably, the mantra of the Reformation, "*soli Deo gloria,*" served as the basis of Bach's conception of music; Bach writes, "The aim and final end of all music should be none other than the glory of God and the refreshment of the soul."[12] For all the spiritual and theological benefits the Christian church has reaped from God's working through Martin Luther and the Reformation, we can thank God for the musical legacy of the Reformation as well. As we thank God for Luther, let us also thank God for Bach. As we strive to make new music for the glory of God and the edification of the church, let's follow Bach's example of immersing our creativity in theologically rich and biblically saturated truths. Let's continue the reforming of Christian music!

---

[11] Dr. Robin Leaver quoted in Wilbur, *Glory and Honor*, 117.
[12] J.S. Bach quoted in Wilbur, *Glory and Honor*, 1.

ON MUSIC
J.S. Bach: "Do all to the glory of God"

This essay examines how Christianity and a Christian worldview were foundational to the creative genius of one of music's greatest composers and musicians, Johann Sebastian Bach.[1]

In 1934, in a Michigan farmhouse, a seventeenth-century German Bible was discovered. What made this finding so remarkable was that the Bible originally belonged to the great Baroque composer, Johann Sebastian Bach.[2] Even more remarkable is the fact that this three-volume edition of the Bible was personally annotated by Bach, containing reflections and responses to specific verses; Bach even made corrections to errors in translation and commentary![3] Robin Leaver writes, "The marginalia and underlinings, written for no one but [Bach] himself, reveal that he was a careful student of the Bible."[4] When Bach died in 1750, an inventory of his personal

---

[1] Previously unpublished essay.
[2] Gregory Wilbur, *Glory and Honor: The Musical and Artistic Legacy of Johann Sebastian Bach* (Nashville: Cumberland House, 2005), 116.
[3] "Johann Sebastian Bach: The Fifth Evangelist" in Mark Galli and Ted Olsen, eds., *131 Christians Everyone Should Know* (Nashville: Holman, 2000), 109.
[4] Dr. Robin Leaver quoted in Wilbur, *Glory and Honor*, 116.

library revealed "an extraordinarily (for the day) large number of ecclesiastical volumes."[5] Such a tangible record of Bach's faith leads one musicologist to write, "Bach the Christian, Bach the believer. To appreciate more fully the character of his music requires that we more fully appreciate the character of his faith."[6]

In the eyes of the world, however, Johann Sebastian Bach is not celebrated for his spirituality; rather, he is noted as the forefather of Western music, holding "the central position" in the history of music.[7] Without Bach, we wouldn't have Mozart, Beethoven or Brahms. Bach was a prolific composer, brilliant organist and an inventive musical genius. His ability to act both as a conservator *and* innovator of music is what places him at the top of the list of musical giants. He excelled at traditional forms of music while expanding and elevating these forms to new heights, achieving the highest realized potential in nearly every style of music known in Bach's day.[8] When Mozart first encountered Bach's music, he was "entranced" by it. According to Harold Schonberg, Mozart studied Bach's compositions, "arranged some music, and was strongly influenced by Bachian counterpoint."[9] Mozart described Bach's music as "music from which a man can learn something." Beethoven and Brahms were also influenced by Bach.[10] Brahms said, "Study Bach: there you will find everything." With brutal honesty, Robert Schuman writes, "Playing and studying Bach convinces us that we are all numbskulls."[11]

With such praise, it is surprising to discover that this musical giant was a humble and gracious man who devoted his life and

---

[5] Harold C. Schonberg, *The Lives of Great Composers* (London: Futura Publications, 1989), 14.
[6] Fr. Martin Shannon, "Soli Deo Gloria," in *The Sacred Choral Music of J.S. Bach*, ed. John Butt (Massachusetts: Paraclete Press, 1997).
[7] Donald Grout, *A History of Western Music* (New York: W.W. Norton & Co., 1973), 435.
[8] Paul Johnson, *Creators: From Chaucer and Dürer to Picasso and Disney* (New York: HarperCollins, 2006), 85.
[9] Schonberg, *The Lives of Great Composers*, 29.
[10] Schonberg, *The Lives of Great Composers*, 29.
[11] Robert Schuman quoted in Wilbur, *Glory and Honor*.

talents to the glory of God.[12] Over three quarters of his astonishing 1,000 compositions consisted of music composed for worship in the church. Some scholars balk at the notion that Bach's perceived Christianity had anything to do with his music.[13] J.S. Bach, however, states plainly that, "The aim and final end of all music should be none other than the glory of God and the refreshment of the soul." The letters "S.D.G." (*soli Deo gloria*—"To God alone be the glory") were inscribed on many of Bach's compositions. He meant this Latin phrase as a testimony—not only to those who would perform his music but also to generations to come—that this music was for God's glory, not Bach's. He strove to live by Paul's words: "Whether you eat or drink or whatever you do, do all to the glory of God" (1 Corinthians 10:31). Even on much of Bach's "secular" compositions, we find inscribed the letters "J.J." (*Jesu, Juva*—"Jesus, help!") or "I.N.J." (*In nomine Jesu*—"In the name of Jesus").[14]

The life, music and legacy of J.S. Bach is a reminder to all Christians to use the gifts and talents God has given us for the glory of God and the building up of his church. For Bach, there was no dichotomy between secular and sacred. Whatever he did, for whatever purpose, he did for his heavenly Father. To God alone be the glory.

Recommended listening:
Sir David Willcocks and The Bach Choir, English version of J.S. Bach's St. Matthew Passion *(based on Matthew 26–27);*
3 CDs, Decca, 2006.
Essential Bach: 36 of His Greatest Masterpieces; 2 CDs, Decca, 2000.

---

[12] Johnson, *Creators*, 82.
[13] Wilbur, *Glory and Honor*, 115–116.
[14] Wilbur, *Glory and Honor*, 225.

ON MUSIC
Handel's masterpiece

This essay examines George Frideric Handel's magnum opus, Messiah, a musical masterpiece that has been continually performed around the globe since its debut over 200 years ago.[1] *Handel demonstrates how music effectively mirrors and conveys the truths described by the lyrics (libretto), which were taken entirely from the Scriptures.*[2]

Have you listened to music lately? We certainly *hear* a great deal of music every day—at the grocery store or shopping mall, over the car radio, during TV commercials—but most of this music is heard as "background noise" and not as a result of focused listening.

God created a universe where beautiful music can be made and played. Though we worship God in many ways, we most

---

[1] Originally published in *Barnabas*, Vol. 2, No. 4 (Fall 2010): 12.
[2] I am indebted here to the insights of a dear friend and musical genius, Gordon Vanderwoude, and to an essay by Philip Yancey titled "Hallelujah!" which appeared in *Christianity Today* on December 15, 1989. Where their influence ends and my ideas begin, it is hard to tell; such is the impact of good mentors! In humble appreciation, I offer this general acknowledgement of credit and heartfelt thanks.

often worship him musically. When selecting or writing hymns and songs for worship, we ought to pay careful attention to the theology of the lyrics. However, we also need to consider carefully the music as well. Both lyrics and the music convey valuable messages and stir the heart to devotion—or distraction—in our worship of God.

Nowhere is this potent combination of sound and sense, melody and meaning, music and lyrics, more evident than in George Frideric Handel's *Messiah* (1741). This masterful composition brilliantly uses texts taken entirely from the Scriptures, and it uses music designed to powerfully convey a powerful message—the gospel of Jesus Christ. Handel's *Messiah* is like a sermon put to music. Handel's friend, Charles Jennens, arranged the *libretto* (text of the *oratorio*) in order to challenge the Deists, rationalists and atheists of his day who opposed the divinity of Christ.[3] When Handel received the *libretto*, he was in ill health and in financial ruin. Yet, the arrangement of Scripture verses inspired him like no other work he set out to compose. In only twenty-four days Handel composed his monumental masterpiece—260 pages of handwritten notes!

The beauty and power of Handel's masterpiece is in the way he weaves the Scriptures and the music together, using the instruments and voices to help convey the meaning of the message. Sometimes this is achieved in simple ways, like the rise and fall of notes in lines such as "Ev'ry mountain (↑) and hill (↑) made low (↓)" and the appropriately vibrating sounds of "crooked" and "rough places" becoming level and smooth-sounding when the vocalist sings "straight" and "plain." Sometimes the music is more complicated, such as contrasts in tempo and tone or the interplay of instruments and voices, as it grapples with the theological tensions between God's holy justice and his love for humanity in Part 1—the Advent portion of the oratorio.

---

[3] "George Frideric Handel: Composer of *Messiah*" in Mark Galli and Ted Olsen, eds., *131 Christians Everyone Should Know* (Nashville: Holman, 2000), 113.

In Part 2—the Easter section—Handel's music vacillates between cheery and sombre tones as the scale of our benefits in Christ is weighed against the cost incurred by our sin: "And with His stripes we are healed." At the astonishing "Hallelujah" chorus concluding Part 2, the tragic reality of the cross becomes a glorious and beautiful celebration of the resurrected and reigning "King of Kings, and Lord of Lords." During the London performance in 1743, King George I stood during this chorus believing the oratorio was over. But like the gospel story, Handel wasn't finished. Part 3 of the work describes the redemption of the world through faith in Jesus Christ. This final part of *Messiah* reminds us that the gospel is not only an historic demonstration of God's transformative power, but the gospel is also a *present reality* of God's transformative power as seen in the church today. In other words, we should come away from Handel's *Messiah* not only moved by the love and sacrifice of Christ but also *empowered* and *renewed*. The chorus in Part 3 declares, "But thanks be to God, who giveth us the victory through our Lord Jesus Christ."

If you have the opportunity to *hear* Handel's *Messiah*, then be sure to *listen* carefully as well: the stunning and glorious music will do more than tickle your ears—it will stir your soul!

V
ON CINEMA

V

ON CINEMA

ON CINEMA
Pitching your tents

This essay provides a guide for Christians to become "film literate"—that is, to show discernment in movie-watching and to exercise critical and biblical thinking when responding to films, without abandoning either the medium or the faith along the way.[1]

In Genesis we read about Lot "pitching his tents toward Sodom" (Genesis 13:12). The next time we read about Lot he is living *in* Sodom, a wicked and abominable city (Genesis 19). We find him applying skewed "righteousness" in an unrighteous situation (19:8), we discover Lot's wife has become too attached to a worldly lifestyle (19:26), his sons-in-law fail to take life seriously (19:14) and his children lack a moral compass (19:30–38). Whatever righteousness Lot had before he went to Sodom was dramatically overshadowed by the unrighteous culture he immersed himself and his family in. As Christians, we are constantly struggling to be *in* the world, but not *of* the world, and it is becoming increasingly difficult to steer clear of "Sodom" these days. Through television, the Internet, movies and magazines, Christians are bombarded by

---

[1] Originally published in *Barnabas*, Vol. 2, No. 1 (Winter 2010): 10.

a culture opposed to the things of God—perhaps the most potent of these cultural influences is Hollywood.

Movies have a significant impact in our society. With drama and realism, movies present a made-for-film world where God's reality—his decrees, his design and his plan—often has no bearing. As a result, social values—the cultural blueprint for the way we interact with each other and with God—are being created, shaped and solidified through the magic of movie-making. Our children, our churches, the people we are trying to reach with the gospel, are all being influenced by movies.

Christians need to become "film literate"—we need to be able to recognize, understand and speak to the filmmaker's message. The challenge is the *subtlety* of the message. Filmmakers aren't literally standing behind a pulpit or on a soapbox preaching their values or their version of the world, but they are saying *something*, and they are saying *it* with millions of dollars, heaps of glitz and pizzazz and great soundtracks. Not all films present non-Christian worldviews. Arguably, some great films are very consistent with the moral laws of God's created universe. There are, however, many films that directly or indirectly oppose God's creation. Sometimes the movies desensitize us to sin, making evil tolerable or even palatable. Sometimes films uphold a right belief, but teach a wrong application. We need to be able to identify what these films are impressing upon us as viewers.

When choosing movies to watch for yourself or your family, you need to do more than count how many expletives or explosions there are. It is not the violence, *per se*, but the *values presented* that make the largest impact on viewers. Movies labelled as "family," for example, may not have a single swear word or a single act of violence, but they may teach that children who disobey their parents are doing the right thing, or that the end justifies the means or that romance is the key to happiness in life. Be prepared to discuss with your family the values presented in the films and contrast them to God's values.

If you are in doubt about whether a movie is OK to watch,

then just don't watch it. If you are watching a film and feel your "tents are pitched too close to Sodom," leave the theatre or turn off the movie. The apostle Paul writes to the Philippians, "Whatever is true, whatever is honorable, whatever is just, whatever is pure, whatever is lovely, whatever is commendable, if there is any excellence, if there is anything worthy of praise, think about these things" (Philippians 4:8).

Where are you pitching *your* tents?

Useful aids for movie viewers: IMDb website provides an online parent guide, and PluggedIn.com (Focus on the Family) provides an excellent Christian guide, with reviews and commentary on movies and television programs. Use these resources to make wise decisions and to be aware of the message being conveyed through this powerful medium.

ON CINEMA
A case for movie-making

This essay argues for Christian filmmakers to make movies that present the gospel and a Christian worldview in new ways to a twenty-first century generation. The Word must always be proclaimed, but film is a means God can use to draw people to his Word.[1]

"What has Hollywood to do with Jerusalem?" Tertullian might ask if he were alive today. This is a good question twenty-first century Christians need to ask. When Tertullian asked his original famous question—"What has Athens to do with Jerusalem?"—he was referring to the practice of applying Greek philosophical methods to Christian theology. However, even Tertullian himself used the achievements of pagan intellectualism to serve Christianity.[2] Francis Schaeffer points out that all truth is God's truth and everything

---

[1] Originally published in *Barnabas*, Vol. 3, No. 4 (Fall 2011): 12.
[2] Everett Ferguson, "Tertullian," in *Introduction to the History of Christianity*, ed. Tim Dowley (Minneapolis: Fortress Press, 2002), 112.

under the sun is under the lordship of Jesus Christ.³ This is why the apostle Paul went to Mars Hill, the philosophical and religious centre of Athens, and he spoke to the people gathered there in the manner of the day—he referenced their gods, their poetry and their way of thinking. The book of Acts records many of the apostles speaking in marketplaces and at religious centres—the places where people gathered. So the question we should ask is this: Where is our Mars Hill in the twenty-first century? If we are going to continue the missionary work of proclaiming the gospel to the culture we live in, we ought to go where people are gathering and where their ideas are being shaped, and we ought to speak to them in a manner they understand. The Word must always be proclaimed, but film can be a means to draw people to that Word. This means that gifted and talented Christians need to enter the world of movie-making.

According to the Motion Picture Association of America (MPAA), over one-billion movie tickets were sold in North America during 2016. MPAA also reports that two thirds (71%) of the combined population of Canada and the US are moviegoers. Movie theatres are where the people are gathering; film is the medium they are listening to and watching. Given the fact that our culture is being powerfully shaped by false worldviews presented in films, Christians need to provide a *counter* worldview, a worldview grounded in the truth of God's created universe.

Since film is a very realistic medium, it lends itself very well to the Christian gospel message. Christianity is no abstract, pie-in-the-sky, philosophical religion. It is a real, gritty, dirt-under-the-fingernails faith. It impacts the lives of real people living in a real world. Film can clearly and powerfully show how the gospel transforms people's lives where they are—in a real, gritty, dirt-under-the-fingernails world. Because of this realism, visual media can be a scary realm for Christians. It pulls us out of our

---

3   This is a major theme in many of the writings of Francis Schaeffer; see, for example, *Art and the Bible* (Downers Grove: InterVarsity Press, 2006).

Christian comfort zone of polished wood pews, "stained-glass and Sunday School associations."[4] But Christianity speaks to the whole world, to its beauty *and* its ugliness. So Christians need to use the advantage God has given them as filmmakers to visually and accurately depict the world as it really is. This includes human suffering, but also human value and meaning. The influence of evil is part of our world, but so is the power of providence and the role of grace. Hollywood rarely portrays the world as it actually is. This is because Hollywood isn't interested in beauty, goodness or truth—it is interested in box office receipts and the bottom line.

God has blessed many Christians with the gifts, talents and technical skills to make good movies. Lately, some very interesting Christian-themed and Christian-made movies have appeared—albeit briefly—in theatres around the world. Granted, there have been some embarrassing and poorly made films over the years as well. Like all things done in the name of Christ, filmmaking should be done with excellence. This excellence should be seen in both the message and medium. In other words, Christians should not only present a right message, but also preserve and perfect the "art" of filmmaking, which includes quality cinematography, inspiring musical scores and authentic performances by actors.

Some would argue that we should not compete with the unbelievers on their turf; but the truth is it's not their turf. The entire world is under the lordship of Jesus Christ. This world is *his* turf. That isn't to say that the many evil films that pour out of Hollywood are ordained by God. We still live in a fallen world, and we are still praying, "Thy will be done." Christians are to be engaged in spiritual warfare; movie theatres are just another battleground where they can wage war not only against temptations,

---

[4] To borrow the concept (and phrase) from C.S. Lewis in his essay "Sometimes Fairy Stories May Say Best What's To Be Said," in *C.S. Lewis Essay Collection: Literature, Philosophy and Short Stories*, ed. Lesley Walmsley (London: HarperCollins, 2002), 120.

distorted worldviews and distractions but also for advancing the truth, beauty and goodness of the gospel.

A Christian-themed film is never a substitute for personal testimony and preaching of the Word. We also know that the Lord uses "the foolish in the world to shame the wise" and he chooses "what is weak in the world to shame the strong" (1 Corinthians 1:27). Nevertheless, a movie can be a starting point for conversations and a means to interest people in the things of God. Movies can also reach the hearts and minds of individuals who would otherwise never set foot in a church building. So, if God is calling you to make a movie in his name, then go and make a great movie. Perhaps the Lord is calling you "for such a time as this" (Esther 4:14).

VI

ON FAITH & CULTURE

ON FAITH & CULTURE
Reforming art

This essay examines the impact of the Protestant Reformation on art. Although the Reformation is often associated with iconoclasm—the destruction of art in cathedrals, churches and monasteries across Europe—the Reformation also contributed positively to the art world by supporting a new emerging art ethos which celebrated the impact of the gospel on everyday life and culture.[1]

The Protestant Reformation began in 1517 in Germany and spread throughout Europe and the world. The Reformation was a theological movement intent on purging unbiblical doctrines, practices and traditions from the Christian faith. In addition to the revolt against Roman Catholic theology, many communities also experienced the removal or zealous destruction of art from places of worship—this included tapestries, statuaries, furniture, stained-glass windows, books, paintings and other forms of religious art. This legacy of destruction—called iconoclasm—often overshadows some of the positive contributions of the Protestant Reformation on art.

---

[1] Originally published in *Barnabas*, Vol. 9, No. 4 (Fall 2017): 14.

The most common misunderstanding about the Reformation's impact on art is a belief that the Reformers were opposed to all kinds of art. This, however, was not case. In *How Should We Then Live?* Francis Schaeffer argues against claims "that the Reformation depreciated art and culture or that it did not produce art and culture;" he calls this view "either nonsense or dishonest."² For example, Martin Luther, one of the principal catalysts of the Reformation, risked imprisonment and even death when he came out of hiding and returned to Wittenberg to stop the destruction of religious art. Luther was also instrumental in ensuring the art of music continued to play an important role in worship, especially through hymnody.

Many Reformers also saw the value of art *outside* the church. In *State of the Arts*, Gene Edward Veith, Jr. argues that Reformers like John Calvin and even extreme iconoclastic Reformer Ulrich Zwingli believed that art has a powerful and enduring role to play in the world. Calvin, for example, writes that "sculpture and paintings are gifts of God," and he desires "a pure and legitimate use of each."³

The fear that art can be a distraction in worship or—worse— lead to idolatry was a pressing concern for Reformers. These are still legitimate concerns when considering the use of art in worship services. However, the most significant result of the Reformed view of art, particularly in Northern Europe, was the rise of masterpieces that addressed non-religious subjects. The scope of subjects addressed by art became larger, and this is due, in part, to the fact that artists were encouraged and empowered to ply their craft in other venues outside the church by addressing a range of topics beyond overtly religious content.

The broadening of art beyond religion is the most significant and unexpected consequence of the Reformation's impact on

---

² Francis A. Schaeffer, *How Should We Then Live?* (Wheaton: Crossway, 2005), 97.
³ Gene Edward Veith, Jr., *State of the Arts: From Bezalel to Mapplethorpe* (Wheaton: Crossway, 1991), 59.

art. Pushing art out of the formal church context into the world gave artists more themes and subjects to explore with their craft. For centuries in Europe, most artists—with few exceptions—worked on religious-themed masterpieces for ecclesiastical use. For example, a portrait of a woman and her baby almost always depicted Mary and the infant Jesus. Portraits of ordinary individuals and of everyday life were rare. When the Reformation exploded on the scene, everyday life became a significant subject for artists. For example, the theological premium Reformers placed on the value of individuals, led to the rise of individual portraiture. The Reformed view of the family resulted in increased paintings of families at home carrying out the activities of daily life. Veith, Jr. points out that as the Reformation took hold, paintings of ordinary people conducting business and living their lives became commonplace. As another scholar notes, the emerging artwork following the Protestant Reformation "reflected the plainer, more unvarnished and more personal Christianity of the Reformation movement."[4]

By pushing art out of the exclusively religious context, a new era of non-religious art ensued. This isn't to say that the art ceased addressing a Christian worldview or that artists stopped portraying religious content. Instead, the Christian worldview began to manifest itself through applications in everyday life—values like the so-called "Protestant work ethic," the importance of family and the transformative effect of the gospel in the lives of individuals. Rembrandt van Rijn (1606–1669), one of the Dutch Masters, often painted biblical scenes with characters dressed in contemporary attire and many depictions of biblical scenes including self-portraits of the artist himself. In Rembrandt's *Raising of the Cross* (c.1633), he includes himself participating in the crucifixion of Christ. Matthew Barrett writes, "Why would Rembrandt place himself at the feet of Jesus as he

---

[4] Neil Collins, "Protestant Reformation Art (c.1520–1700)," *Encyclopedia of Art History*, http://www.visual-arts-cork.com/history-of-art/protestant.htm#reformationart

is being hoisted up and crucified? For no other reason than to tell the world that Rembrandt is a sinner and it was his sins, like the rest of mankind, which sent Christ to the cross."[5] The implication of this approach is to bring the gospel message to present-day life—we are *all* sinners saved by grace. This is one of the greatest legacies of the Reformation on the world of the arts.

Without a doubt, art and religion are inextricably linked—this can be seen not only in Christian contexts but in religious art from around the world: countless paintings, sculptures and furnishings have been inspired by and used for religious purposes. Artistic endeavours and religious pursuits both compliment and augment each other because both art and religion attempt to communicate the transcendent and supernatural realities of the universe—the sublime, the infinite, the abstract. As useful as art is in aiding in worship, the Reformation helped us to see the merits of art beyond the walls of cathedrals and stained-glass windows. The Reformation brought art, along with the gospel, to our everyday lives.

---

[5] Matthew Barrett, "Raising the Cross," *CREDO* (September 24, 2011), http://www.credomag.com/2011/09/24/raising-the-cross/

ON FAITH & CULTURE
Darwin & the shrivelling of our artistic "soul"

This essay examines the "decline of art" in the Western world, attributing this to the rise of evolutionary theory and the application of Darwinism to all areas of the human experience. [1]

During the nineteenth century, Europe witnessed the creation of some of the most imaginative and innovative forms of art. Consider the musical masterpieces of Beethoven, Haydn and Mendelssohn...the poetry of Keats, Wordsworth and Coleridge...the novels of Austen, Dickens and Dostoyevsky... the art of Goya, Renoir and van Gogh. By the twentieth century, the arts began to lessen in significance and ingenuity. Artists abdicated their responsibility to convey truth, beauty and goodness to their readers, viewers and listeners. One of the most influential catalysts for this decline was the emergence of Darwinism. By rejecting the Great Artist, all artists and art began to fade. By rejecting the Great Author, all authors diminished in relevance and worth. By rejecting *the* Book, all books diminished in importance and value. It is no surprise that Charles Darwin

---

[1] Originally published in *Barnabas*, Vol. 4, No. 4 (Fall 2012): 14.

noted in his autobiography a similar dwindling of his personal appreciation of the arts:

> Up to the age of 30 or beyond it, poetry of many kinds... gave me great pleasure, and even as a schoolboy I took intense delight in Shakespeare.... Formerly pictures gave me considerable—and music very great—delight. But now for many years I cannot endure to read a line of poetry: I have tried to read Shakespeare, and found it so intolerably dull that it nauseated me. I have also almost lost any taste for pictures or music.... I retain some taste for fine scenery, but it does not cause me the exquisite delight which it formerly did.... My mind seems to have become a kind of machine for grinding general laws out of large collections of facts, but why this should have caused the atrophy of that part of the brain alone, on which the higher tastes depend, I cannot conceive.... The loss of these tastes is a loss of happiness, and may possibly be injurious to the intellect, and more probably to the moral character, by enfeebling the emotional part of our nature.[2]

Darwin's personal testimony was a forecast of what—on a larger scale—Western culture was to experience in the ensuing decades after the publication of his *On the Origin of Species*. As Western civilization embraced Darwinian evolution, not only did its spiritual "soul" shrivel, so did its artistic "soul." Artists began to view Creation, with all of its wonder, beauty and design, simply as a result of "random chance" and "natural selection." Consequently their art became increasingly random, meaningless, anti-conventional and unrefined, defying beliefs and opposing beauty. Indiscriminate piles of material, corroding metals and haphazard paint splatters—all of this replaced the skilful

---

[2] Charles Darwin as quoted in John Piper, *Desiring God* (Sisters: Multinomah Books, 1996), 88–89.

artistry, design and meaning of previous centuries.[3] Art was no longer about order, but rather about chaos. Both in content and form, art reflected the new belief that God's created universe was a chaotic wilderness, a Darwinian desert. Even though the Fall has marred Creation and humanity, God's grace still allows glimpses of paradise and beauty, both in nature and in human creativity. James tells us, "Every good and perfect gift is from above, coming down from the Father" (James 1:17). God gave us so much to *delight* in. Christians must rise above our Darwin-infused culture, where art is all but extinct. Defy Darwin and delight in art.

---

[3] Lest I seem too heavy-handed or hyperbolic, it is worth noting that there is much twentieth-century and twenty-first-century art that contains "excellence" and "beauty" in spite of the pervasive Darwinian worldview in the Western world. In praise of modern artistic achievements, Dr. Peter Pikkert asks "Who conveys the loneliness of city life better than, say, Edward Hopper, or crass capitalist materialism than Andy Warhol? Who portrays wildlife better than Bateman? Or the Canadian wilderness than the Group of Seven? Which painting portrays the horror of war better than Picasso's *Guernica*? Or poignancy and the value of a human life, even when invalided, than Andrew Wyeth's *Christina's World*? ...The twentieth century has seen great works of humanizing literature, amazing music, film, etc." (Dr. Peter Pikkert, email to author, August 19, 2017).

ON FAITH & CULTURE
What about nudity in art?

This essay examines nudity in art and the Christian's response to it. Does nudity in art make it pornographic? Should Christian artists avoid depicting the naked human form in their work? Should Christian appreciators of art be wary of nudity in paintings and sculptures?[1]

Strolling through an art gallery or flipping through a book of artistic masterpieces, you will likely encounter nudity in paintings and sculptures. Does nudity in art make it pornographic? What should Christian artists and art appreciators do with nudity in art? Is the portrayal of the naked human form something we ought to "flee" (2 Timothy 2:22)?

Christian art historian Hans Rookmaaker notes that nudity is found in every period of Western art.[2] This is not surprising. Like all aspects of God's creation, the naked human form—in its ideal and healthy state—is beautiful and glorious; this is why

---

[1] A shorter, edited version of this essay was published in *Barnabas*, Vol. 10, No. 1–2 (Winter/Spring 2018): 12.
[2] H.R. Rookmaaker, *Modern Art and The Death of Culture* (Wheaton: Crossway, 1994), 239.

so many artists seek to depict and celebrate this beauty in their art. The Bible, however, shows us that clothing—and the *lack* of clothing—have significant meaning. When Adam and Eve sinned, their eyes "were opened, and they knew that they were naked" (Genesis 3:7). This awareness of nudity was not a liberating experience for Adam and Eve: instead, they immediately attempted to cover their exposed weakness and shame by sewing fig leaves and making loincloths. They also attempted to hide from God because of their nakedness (Genesis 3:10). The Bible consistently presents nakedness as shameful (Genesis 9:23; Exodus 20:26; Isaiah 20:4; 47:3; Ezekiel 16:36; 23:29; Nahum 3:5; Habakkuk 2:16; Revelation 3:18). The only exceptions are in Eden before the Fall, when "Adam and his wife were both naked, and they felt no shame" (Genesis 2:25), and in the context of marriage (Song of Songs 5:10–16; 7:1–9; Proverbs 5:18–19). Unredeemed human beings, as noble and glorious as we may sometimes appear, still "fall short of the glory of God" (Romans 3:23). This is why Christian artists who have used nudity in their art intentionally do so to express the feebleness and vulnerability of humanity. For example, among notably pious artists like Rembrandt and Dürer, nudity means humanity in its weakness, which is consistent with the biblical perspective.[3]

Is a biblical perspective on nudity sufficient to differentiate nudity in art from pornography? Shouldn't we still make a "covenant with our eyes" and avoid viewing art that portrays nakedness (Job 31:1)? Pornography seems like art, but they are in fact polar opposites. What distinguishes pornography from art is not whether it contains nudity or sexual activity but in the *way* it depicts the body and sexuality: pornography is the degrading and gratuitous portrayal of nudity and sex acts, which is designed to elicit an erotic reaction from the audience. The dividing line is whether or not the nudity or sexual content is intended to evoke a titillating and erotic response that leads to

---

[3] Rookmaaker, *Modern Art and The Death of Culture*, 239.

lust and committing adultery in the heart (Matthew 5:28). Can realistic portrayals of nudity or sex ever *not be* provocative? The Bible depicts all aspects of the human experience realistically; this includes nudity and sexual activity. Jerram Barrs points out that the Song of Songs—albeit in slightly veiled poetic language—"contains explicit descriptions of nudity and of very sensual sex" within the context of marital love.[4] In other places as well, the Scriptures unabashedly refer to sexual activity within marriage (Genesis 1:28; 4:1; 30:16; Ruth 4:13; 2 Samuel 12:24). The Bible also contains a full range of realistic—albeit non-gratuitous—portrayals of sexual immorality: a sampling of sexually charged topics covered in the Bible are prostitution (Genesis 38:15; Judges 16:1), rape (Genesis 34), homosexual conduct (Genesis 19:4-9; Romans 1; 2 Peter 2:6-10; Jude 7), debauchery (Exodus 32:6, 19, 25), sexual violence (Judges 19:22-30), incest (2 Samuel 13; 1 Corinthians 5:1), voyeurism (2 Samuel 11:2-3) and adultery (Genesis 39:6-19; 2 Samuel 11:2-5). None of these accounts make the Word of God pornographic.

In its treatment of nudity, sex and sexual immorality, Leland Ryken argues that the "Bible strikes a balance. It gives us realism within certain bounds."[5] Ryken points out that the Bible doesn't dwell on the details—lingering on nakedness or sexual activity; it isn't central or excessive in its coverage of the erotic aspects of life and the Bible never condones the immoral behaviour it describes.[6] The Bible's approach to these topics can serve as a helpful guide for how Christian artists should deal with these subjects. Nevertheless, the most challenging medium for addressing nudity and sexual activity in a moderate and biblical way is the visual arts, where unintended provocation is more likely to occur.

---

[4] Jerram Barrs, *Echoes of Eden: Reflections on Christianity, Literature, and the Arts* (Wheaton: Crossway, 2013), 60.
[5] Leland Ryken, *The Liberated Imagination: Thinking Christianly About the Arts* (Eugene: Wipf & Stock, 2005), 242.
[6] Ryken, *The Liberated Imagination*, 242.

Can nudity ever be a safe subject for Christian visual artists? It is important to note that the incarnation of Christ reminds us that Christianity is a religion of the body as much as it is of the soul. A low view of the body has often led to destructive heresies in the Christian church (for example, Gnosticism; the church's low view of the body also opened the door to other non-Christian influences such as Manichaeism and Neoplatonism). Topics like nudity and sexuality, when viewed with a biblical perspective, are important for Christian artists—as well as preachers and teachers—to address in their work. Caution and care, however, should always be used. Paul warns Christians, for the sake of the church, to be careful how they exercise their liberty in Christ: "But take care that this right of yours does not somehow become a stumbling block to the weak" (1 Corinthians 8:9). There are modern Christian artists who have used nudity to meaningful effect, but it is still a controversial artistic decision that should not be taken lightly.[7] Also, no amount of skill or aesthetic beauty can justify a work of art that is clearly pornographic or highly offensive to those who seriously desire to set their "minds on things that are above, not on things that are on earth" (Colossians 3:2).

In spite of the artist's *intention* for benign use of nudity, appreciators of art may be concerned that such depictions may still be *personally* provocative. What if you find yourself struggling with lust after viewing a painting or sculpture of a nude man or woman? The simple answer is to avoid art galleries or books about art altogether. It is true that you should not unduly tempt yourself in an area of personal weakness. This approach, however, is ultimately only a Band-Aid fix. Attempting to avoid anything that is potentially provocative fails to address the root cause of illicit sexual desire. The sin of lust comes "from within," as Jesus tells us: "For from within, out of the heart of man, come evil thoughts, sexual immorality, theft, murder, adultery, coveting,

---

[7] For further discussion of how contemporary Christian artists have handled nudity in art, see Gene Edward Veith, Jr.'s examination of Edward Knippers in his book *State of the Arts: From Bezalel to Mapplethorpe* (Wheaton: Crossway, 1991), 175–180.

wickedness, deceit, sensuality, envy, slander, pride, foolishness. All these evil things come from within, and they defile a person" (Mark 7:21–23). Christians ought to be cautious about blaming nudity in art for their struggle with lust. Shifting blame from oneself is a common tendency for human beings. For example, when Adam and Eve sinned in the Garden of Eden, they immediately blamed everyone else but themselves (Genesis 3:12–13). Our hearts—not our surroundings—are the root of the problem.

Our hearts need to be transformed and renewed by the Saviour. Trying to control lust with legalism is futile. We need to stop *focusing* on the sin, and instead focus on Christ. We need to fill our vision with him and leave no room for evil. As Paul tells us in Romans, we need to clothe ourselves with the Lord Jesus Christ, and "not think about how to gratify the desires of the sinful nature" (Romans 13:14). This is the simple—yet powerful—reality of the gospel of Jesus Christ.

Without a doubt, dealing with nudity and sexuality in art—and in life!—is a difficult subject. In the secularized Western world, Christian artists and art appreciators need to navigate the biblical road between two extremes: on one side, there is nineteenth-century Victorian prudishness and its lingering hypocrisies, and on the other side, there is the 1960s sexual revolution, which set-off a relentless avalanche of so-called "sexual liberties" still wreaking havoc today.

As the Western world becomes more multicultural and diverse, society is also being inundated with more competing views of what is appropriate and acceptable to include in art. Hans Rookmaaker points out that modesty is expressed differently in different cultures and societies.[8] What may be erotic in one context is entirely mundane in another time or place. If a Christian artist wants to be culturally relevant, then he or she must not only be obedient to biblical principles but also be responsive to the ever-changing landscape of cultural sensitivities.

---

[8] Rookmaaker, *Modern Art and The Death of Culture*, 240.

If you are going to create or appreciate art, apart from wearing blinders in an art gallery, tearing out pages from an art book or blotting out private parts with a magic marker, there is little you can do to avoid it. The point is, there isn't a steadfast rule to measure the appropriateness of a work of art. We need to exercise personal discernment and allow ourselves to be guided by biblical principles. Christian artists should also seek feedback from other trusted brothers and sisters in the Lord, who can provide helpful perspectives on the appropriateness of a given piece of artwork. Most importantly, Christian artists and art appreciators must prayerfully tap into Spirit-led wisdom offered to believers. James tells us that "If any of you lacks wisdom, let him ask God, who gives generously to all without reproach, and it will be given him" (James 1:5).

ON FAITH & CULTURE
Bridging old & new traditions

This essay considers the importance of upholding old traditions only so far as they continue to advance Christ's mission in a biblical way for his church. Likewise, new "traditions" ought to be embraced if they will serve Christ's church today in a better, yet still biblical, way. The key question isn't which tradition or new idea do we prefer; rather, it is: What must we do to continue making known the greatness of God in our current time and place?[1]

Churches are slow to embrace new ideas—and rightly so. The traditions of the church are important; they connect us to our heritage, they provide us with a historical perspective on our own time and they remind us of past solutions to past problems. Before we discard or alter a tradition, we need to understand "why" our faithful predecessors established what they established—what challenges were these traditions originally designed to overcome? Sometimes when we remove an old solution—now tradition—we end up bringing back old problems long since forgotten and long since solved by that tradition. Many traditions, in fact,

---

[1] Originally published in *Barnabas*, Vol. 7, No. 3 (Summer 2015): 14.

are worth keeping and preserving because they still serve the church. Some traditions, however, simply preserve practices from a different time and place, turning churches into Christian museums rather than gospel lighthouses. We may prefer our traditions, but tradition should never be followed at the expense of biblical truth or the building up of the church in her present day and age.

A desire to preserve traditions can make some Christians reluctant to embrace new ideas. Ironically, many traditions that we currently preserve were once controversial innovations at some point in church history. One example is the hymns written by Isaac Watts (1674–1748): Watts set out to create new English hymns that speak clearly of Christ and his work. He noticed a lack of connection between the songs his congregation sang and the "fervency of their inward religion."[2] So he paraphrased many of the Psalms using New Testament language, and he wrote new songs using expressions and tunes familiar to the people of his own time and place. Watts wanted to write hymns that were "within the reach of ordinary Christians," which "might easily and naturally be accommodated to various occasions of Christian life."[3] Watts' hymns, however, were considered by some opponents as "flights of fancy"; the hymns were deemed unworthy of pious worship, as some congregations still argue today. The controversy surrounding Watts' new hymns—disapprovingly dubbed "Watts' whims"—resulted in church splits, pastor firings and other forms of discord.[4] In the twenty-first century, however, most Christians would rarely refer to Watts' hymns as too informal or newfangled!

Creating new ideas for the church—like Isaac Watts once did—often means pushing the boundaries of what we are used

---

[2] "Isaac Watts: Father of English Hymnody" in Mark Galli and Ted Olsen, eds., *131 Christians Everyone Should Know* (Nashville: Holman, 2000), 154.
[3] David Fountain, *Isaac Watts Remembered* (Great Britain: Gospel Standard Baptist Trust, 1978), 58.
[4] Galli and Olsen, eds., *131 Christians Everyone Should Know*, 156.

to and what we consider normal. Churches have wrestled with new approaches to all aspects of church life: worship, church programs, outreach, preaching and leadership structure. New ideas, whether they are biblically acceptable or not, often come with discord.

The church, however, cannot allow an aversion for "new" to sidetrack her from effectively presenting biblical truth to our present culture. We must distinguish actual biblical *mandates* from church *traditions* and personal *preferences*. All three have merit, but ultimately, only biblical mandates have authority and only biblical truth is timeless. In the areas of church traditions and personal preferences, we need to be open to embracing news ways of presenting old truths "for such a time as this" (Esther 4:14). Whether we create new "traditions," like new songs, new music or new art, we must clearly convey the transforming truth and beauty of Christ to the time and place God has called us to serve.

What traditions continue to advance the mission of the church, which is to be Christ's witness "to the ends of the earth" (Acts 1:8)? Are new "traditions" needed? What old traditions hinder the mission? Christ did not die for Christian museums; he died for the church. What has God called your church to be?

ON FAITH & CULTURE
The beautiful cross

This essay considers the role, if any, ornate and beautiful crosses have in adorning our homes, places of worship and our jewellery. Are we diminishing the horrors of the historical cross or are we conveying a gospel message of a redeemed instrument of death and our new means to life eternal? [1]

Strolling through a Christian bookstore, one cannot help but notice the array of gilded and adorned crosses for sale. Is there a place for these sorts of "dressed up" symbols of Christ's crucifixion in our homes and places of worship? If we have a cross on display at all, shouldn't we only exhibit a realistic wooden cross to emphasize the historical reality of the death and resurrection of Jesus? Is a decorated and symbolic cross just kitschy sugar-coating that obscures the horrors of the historical cross? We sing hymns and songs about the beauty of the cross: the old rugged cross is made attractive by the melody of many hymns and the poetry of the lyrics. Preachers and authors have often waxed poetic about the beauty of the cross, yet we are uncertain about

---

[1] Originally published in *Barnabas*, Vol. 8, No. 1–2 (Winter/Spring 2016): 14.

presenting the cross as *visually* beautiful. Is there a role to play for beautiful crosses?

Author and preacher Timothy Keller states, "Art is often a back door to truth" because it involves "a movement from the right brain to the left."[2] This is why art has always played a prominent role in the body of Jesus Christ, whether through music, visual art, poetry or even eloquent preaching (for example, C.H. Spurgeon, who was known as the "Poet Preacher").[3] Christianity speaks to the whole person—our body, soul, heart and mind. Churches, however, sometimes put the emphasis only on *left-brain* cerebral Christianity. But art, especially visual art, puts emphasis on our *right-brain* thinking as well as our emotional centre. Art attempts to capture and convey *abstract* truths in symbolically and emotionally provocative ways.

Over the centuries, artists have presented the abstract truth about the *beauty* of the cross by transforming an ugly, Roman instrument of torture and death into a physically beautiful piece of art. "O death, where is your sting?" the apostle Paul asks (1 Corinthians 15:55). The artistic transformation of the cross is intended to show that we have no fear or revulsion for the cross as an instrument of execution. Jesus has made the cross attractive to a believer's heart and mind. Humanity's most hideous and repulsive act of evil—the historical crucifixion of Christ upon the cross—became God's great and beautiful act of love and redemption for humanity. What the artistically beautified cross does is visually convey the biblical truth about what Christ has done *spiritually* and *physically* (i.e., in time and space): he has taken a horrific and ugly instrument of death and made it beautiful.

---

[2] Timothy Keller, "Worship Worthy of the Name," *Christianity Today*, 1995, http://www.christianitytoday.com/pastors/books/preachingworship/lclead01-18.html.

[3] For an excellent examination of the eloquence and artfulness of preaching, see Cyril Guérette's essay "The Pastor as Poet" in *For Christ and His Church: Essays in Service of the Church and Its Mission* (Kitchener: Joshua Press, 2015), 53–60.

If, in the wisdom and providence of God, Jesus came to earth in a different century, the mode of execution might have been an electric chair or a hangman's gallows. Would we do the same thing to these instruments of death as many Christians have done with the cross? Would we wear a gilded and adorned electric chair on a necklace or hang an ornate noose on our wall? The answer would be yes. The electric chair would look like a throne because Jesus' lordship and triumph over death makes it a throne. The ugly, dark and sorrowful mode of execution would become a beautiful source of life, light and joy; it would still be "a stumbling block to the Jew and folly to the Gentile," but to a believer in Jesus Christ, it would be a glorious and beautiful thing (1 Corinthians 1:23–25).

Through his death and resurrection, Jesus turns the rough-hewn wooden cross into a canvas upon which he uses his blood to paint a magnificent portrait of his great act of love. Over the centuries, artists have laboured to use their gifts to express this beautification of the cross in artistic form. The rough-hewn cross still has a role to play, reminding us not only of the ugliness and shame of the cross but also the historicity of the cross—that the crucifixion was a *real* event on a *real* instrument of death. But the beautified cross is important too, showing us that our Great God "makes all things new" (Revelations 21:5), and he works all things "together for good" (Romans 8:28), and that although Christ "endured the cross, despising the shame," he is now "seated at the right hand of the throne of God" (Hebrews 12:2).

Perhaps the beautified cross is the artists' way of symbolizing our paradoxical love for the cross. The apostle Paul sums it up well when he writes, "But far be it from me to boast except in the cross of our Lord Jesus Christ, by which the world has been crucified to me, and I to the world" (Galatians 6:14). Whether your cross is wooden or gilded, let us boast in our beautiful cross, made wonderful by the Great Artist's hand.

For further reading

Barrs, Jerram. *Echoes of Eden: Reflections on Christianity, Literature, and the Arts*. Wheaton: Crossway, 2013.
Dickenson, Matthew, and David O'Hara. *From Homer to Harry Potter: A Handbook on Myth and Fantasy*. Grand Rapids: Brazos Press, 2006.
Lewis, C.S. *An Experiment in Criticism*. Cambridge: Canto, 2004.
———. *Image and Imagination*. Edited by Walter Hooper. Cambridge: Canto, 2013.
Peters, Thomas C. *The Christian Imagination: G.K. Chesterton on the Arts*. San Francisco: Ignatius Press, 2000.
Rookmaaker, Hans R. *Art Needs No Justification*. Vancouver: Regent College Publishing, 2010.
———. *Modern Art and the Death of Culture*. Wheaton: Crossway, 1994.
Ryken, Leland, ed. *The Christian Imagination: The Practice of Faith in Literature and Writing*. Colorado Springs: Shaw Books, 2005.
———. *The Liberated Imagination: Thinking Christianly About the Arts*. The Wheaton Literary Series. Wheaton: Harold Shaw, 1989.
———. *Realms of Gold: The Classics in Christian Perspective*. Wheaton: Harold Shaw, 1991.

Ryken, Philip Graham. *Art for God's Sake*. Phillipsburg: P&R Publishing, 2006.

Sayers, Dorothy. *The Lost Tools of Learning and The Mind of the Maker*. Oxford: Oxford City Press, 2010.

Schaeffer, Francis A. *Art and the Bible*. Downers Grove: InterVarsity Press, 2006.

Veith, Gene Edward, Jr. *State of the Arts: From Bezalel to Mapplethorpe*. Wheaton: Crossway, 1991.

Scripture index

Genesis		20:26	126	12:24	127
1:28	xx, 127	25–28	20n	13	127
2:9	12, 50	28:33	4		
2:19	34	31	16, 38	1 Kings	
2:25	126	31:4	4	8:27–30	20
3:7	126	31:5	5	8:65	23
3:10	126	31:1–11	3		
3:12–13	129	32	16	1 Chronicles	
4:1	127	32:6, 19, 25	127	28:11–12	12
4:20–22	45n	35:10	42	29:11	xvi
9:8–17	12				
9:23	126	Deuteronomy		2 Chronicles	
13:12	107	8:3	24	3–4	20n
19:3	23			3:6–17	12
19:4–9	127	Judges		5:13	95
19:8	107	14:17	23		
19:14	107	16:1	127	Esther	
19:26	107	19:22–30	127	1:3	23
19:30–38	107			4:14	38, 114, 133
26:30	23	Ruth			
29:22	23	4:13	127	4:16	39
30:16	127				
34	127	2 Samuel		Job	
38:15	127	11	85	31:1	126
39:6–19	127	11:2–3	127		
		11:2–5	127	Psalms	
Exodus		12	64	34:8	25
3:8	23	12:7	85	46:10	60

141

119:103   24
139:13–16   38, 50

Proverbs
5:18–19   126
22:29   49
23:20–21   23
27:9   xxii
27:17   xvi

Ecclesiastes
9:10   42

Song of Songs
5:10–16   126
7:1–9   126

Isaiah
20:4   126
25:6   24
47:3   126
52:7   13

Ezekiel
16:36   126
23:29   126

Daniel
5:1   23

Nahum
3:5   126

Habakkuk
2:16   126

Matthew
5:13–16   xix
5:28   127
9:36   28
16:5–7   8
22:2   24
25:14–30   49
26–27   99n

28:19   43

Mark
7:21–23   129
8:2   28
12:31   27

Luke
7:13   28
10:25–37   28

John
6:35   24
6:48   24

Acts
1:8   133
17:11   55
17:16–34   xvi
17:28   80

Romans
1:18–21   xvi, 127
3:23   126
8:13   73
8:28   137
10:15   13
12:15   30
13:14   129

1 Corinthians
1:23–25   137
1:27   114
3:21–23   xvii
5:1   127
8:9   128
10:3   24
10:31   5, 41, 99
15:55   136

Ephesians
2:10   43, 47
4:28   43
5:15–16   63

Colossians
3:2   128
3:5   73
3:17   89
3:23   42

1 Thessalonians
4:11   88
4:11–12   43

2 Thessalonians
3:12   43

2 Timothy
2:22   125

Hebrews
4:15   28
5:11–14   24
12:2   137
13:3   28

James
1:5   130
1:13   24
1:17   24, 123
1:23–24   73

1 Peter
2:2   24

2 Peter
2:6–10   127

1 John
3:18   89

Jude
7   127

Revelation
3:18   126
19:7–9   24
21:5   137

Index

Adam and Eve xix, xx, 34, 126, 129
aesthetics ii, xxiv, 13, 128
allegory 75-76
analogous 7, 37
Ark of the Covenant 20
ars gratia artis (art for art's sake) 41
art
   by non-Christians xvii, 108, 113
   for evangelism 42, 51, 108, 114
   for worship 3-4, 12, 15-17, 42, 46,
      94-95, 99, 102, 117-118, 120,
      132
   inside the church 12,13, 15-17,
      20, 38, 45-47, 53-55, 60, 95-96,
      99, 117-119, 132-133, 136
   kinds: abstract 19, 20
   kinds: representational art 4, 19,
      20, 76
   kinds: symbolic art 4, 19, 20-21,
      135-137
   subjects for Christian artists 17,
      42-43, 53-55, 118-119, 125-130,
      131-133, 135-137
artistic ability, calling and gift of
   God xii, 3-5, 16, 33-35, 37-39,
   41-45, 46-47, 49-51, 55
Athens xvii, 80, 111-112
Augustine xv-xvi

Austen, Jane 87-89, 121

Bach, Johann Sebastian 45-47,
   93-99
barista 35
Barrs, Jerram xxi, 29, 127, 139
Bateman, Robert 123n
beauty 4, 11-13, 20, 33, 35, 61, 80,
   108, 113, 122, 126, 128, 135-136
Beethoven, Ludwig van 45, 93, 98,
   121
Beowulf 71, 73
Bezalel
   calling of 3-5
   works of 16-17
Bilbo (character from *The Hobbit*)
   71
Bradstreet, Anne 61
Brahms, Johannes 93, 98
Bunyan, John 45, 68, 75-77

Calvin, John xv, 45, 118
Chesterton, G.K. xxi
Chronicles of Narnia, The 67-69, 75
creativity 4, 7-9, 24, 29, 34-35, 39,
   49-50, 53-54, 64-65, 80, 94, 123,
Crosby, Fanny 45, 50n
culinary arts 19, 21, 25

143

Darth Vadar (character from
    Star Wars) 71
Darwinism 121–123
Dickens, Charles 121
Dickenson, Emily 55n
deism, deists 102
delight xiii, xvii, 4, 12, 24, 29, 49,
    64, 69, 77, 88–89, 122
Disney 68
Donne, John 61
dragon 71, 72
Dürer, Albrecht 126

Eliot, T.S. 61
epic poetry 63, 71, 73
Esther 37–39
evil 42, 63, 69, 71–73, 108, 113,
    128–129, 136
ex nihilo 33

fairy tales 71, 72
fallen world iii, 80–81, 88, 113
fantasy novels 67–69
fashion 13, 43
fiction xii, 63–65, 76, 84
film ii, iv, xviii, xxii, 27, 29, 67, 71,
    87, 107–109, 111–119, 123n
filmmakers 38, 43, 108, 111–119
florist 35
friendship xxiii, 8, 27

Garden of Eden xix, 126, 129
golden calf 17
Gollum (character from
    The Hobbit) 71
gospel of Jesus Christ xii, xv–xvi,
    xix, xxii–xxiii, 7–8, 37, 51, 68, 80,
    102–103, 108, 111–112, 114, 117,
    119, 120, 129, 132, 135
Gospels (New Testament books) 8,
    28
Greek philosophical methods 111
Grendel (character from *Beowulf*)
    71

Group of Seven 123n
Grudem, Wayne 4

Handel, George Frideric 101–103
Harry Potter series iii, 67–68, 71
Herbert, George 61
hero 71, 73, 80
Herrick, Robert 61
Hobbit, The 71
Homer, *The Odyssey* 77
Hopper, Edward 123n
hymns, hymnody ii, viii, 4, 13, 34,
    45, 47, 50, 51, 60–61, 95, 102, 118,
    132, 135

iconoclasm, iconoclasts 16, 117–118
idolatry, idols 15–17, 118
imagination xiii, 7–9, 21, 28, 30, 33,
    55n, 63–64, 81, 83, 86

Keller, Timothy xix, xx, xvi, 15, 34,
    35, 136
Kinkade, Thomas 88
Knippers, Edward 128n

L'Abri (the shelter) iv, xix
Leithart, Peter J. xvii, xxi, 81, 89
L'Engle, Madeleine 68
Lennon, John 7
Lewis, C.S. xxi, 29, 30, 45, 54, 63,
    68, 69, 72, 75, 76, 88
Liddell, Eric 50
Lord of the Rings, The 67, 68, 77
Luther, Martin 16, 93–96, 118

Macdonald, George 68
Mars Hill (Areopagus) xvi, 80, 112
medieval art 11, 15, 20
Milton, John 61
modernism xviii, 12, 20, 123n
Mozart, Amadeus 93, 98
musician xxii, 35, 38, 43, 45, 46, 49,
    51, 94, 97

new-age spiritualism 69
nudity 125–130
  in art 125–130
  in the Bible 126–127

Oholiab 3–4

parable 28, 49, 64, 83, 85
Picasso, Pablo 123n
Pikkert, Peter ii, 29, 55n, 123n
Pilgrim's Progress, The iii, 45, 75–77
Piper, John xxi, 9, 51
poetry ii, iii, xii, 5, 45, 54, 59–61, 63, 79, 80, 112, 121, 122, 135, 136
Pollack, Jackson 20
pornography xviii, 126
  as opposed to art 126
  defined 126
postmodernism xviii, 11n, 80
preaching as an art form 136
Pride and Prejudice 87, 89
Pullman, Philip, *The Golden Compass* 69

rationalists 102
realism 108, 112, 127
redeem, redemption iii, xviii, xix–xx, 73, 76, 95, 103, 126, 135–136
Reformation 16, 93–96, 117–120
Rembrandt 119–120, 126
Rookmaaker, H.R. xi–xii, 125, 129
Rossetti, Christina 61
Ryken, Leland iv, xxi, 77, 127
Ryken, Philip xxi, 3n, 41n

Sayers, Dorothy L. xxi, 21
Schaeffer, Edith xix
Schaeffer, Francis xvi, xxi, 8, 12, 13, 29, 38, 64, 111, 118
Screwtape Letters, The 45
secular and sacred divide 42
sermon xxiii, 34, 64, 102
sexual activity 126–128
  in art 126, 129
  in marriage 127
  in the Bible 127
sexual immorality 127–128
  in art 127–128
  in the Bible 127
Shakespeare, William vii, 61, 76, 79–81, 83–86, 122
Shaw, George Bernard 75, 76
Skywalker, Luke (character from *Star Wars*) 71
Spenser, Edmund 61, 68
spiritual warfare 113
Spurgeon, Charles H., 75, 76, 136
  "The Poet Preacher" 136
  on *The Pilgrim's Progress* 75, 76
symbols, symbolism 4, 19, 20–21, 76, 135–137

Tabernacle 3, 5, 20, 42, 46
talent xii, xxii, 4, 37–39, 45–47, 49–51, 99, 112–113
taste 23–25, 95, 122
Temple 12, 20
Tolkien, J.R.R. xxi, 68, 71, 77
tradition ii, iv, xi, 11n, 53, 54, 98, 117, 131–133
truth xv, xvi–xviii, 12, 111, 133
  in art 4–5, 9, 16–17, 51, 95, 121, 136
  in stories 64, 68, 76, 80, 85

Veith, Jr., Gene Edward xviii, xxi, 20, 118–119
Voldemort (character from the *Harry Potter* book and film series) 71
Voyage of the Dawn Treader, The 72

Warhol, Andy 123n
Watts, Isaac 45, 132
Western culture xviii, 59, 93, 98, 121–122, 125, 129
Wilberforce, William 50

worldview xi–xii, xviii, 8, 20, 37–38, 42, 68, 79, 97, 108, 111–112, 114, 119, 123n

worship 3–4, 12, 13, 15–16, 34, 42, 94–95, 99, 101–102, 118, 120, 132–133

Wyeth, Andrew 123n

Zwingli, Ulrich 118

About the author

JEREMY W. JOHNSTON is a teacher of English and classical studies at Hillfield Strathallan College and a professor of communications at Mohawk College. He holds a master's degree in education and an honours degree in English literature and humanities from the University of Western Ontario. He is the arts columnist for *Barnabas* magazine, which is published by the Sovereign Grace Fellowship of Canada. He has been involved in Christian education—teaching, preaching and speaking—at local churches and Christian venues for many years. Jeremy and his wife, Laurie, have been homeschooling their four children for over 15 years. They live in Hamilton, Ont., Canada.

Deo Optimo et Maximo Gloria
To God, best and greatest, be glory

www.joshuapress.com

www.ingramcontent.com/pod-product-compliance
Lightning Source LLC
LaVergne TN
LVHW090115080426
835507LV00040B/895